THE ART OF WOODWORKING

ENCYCLOPEDIA OF WOOD

THE ART OF WOODWORKING

ENCYCLOPEDIA OF WOOD

TIME-LIFE BOOKS
ALEXANDRIA, VIRGINIA

ST. REMY PRESS
MONTREAL • NEW YORK

THE ART OF WOODWORKING was produced by
ST. REMY PRESS

PUBLISHER	Kenneth Winchester
PRESIDENT	Pierre Léveillé
Series Editor	Pierre Home-Douglas
Series Art Director	Francine Lemieux
Senior Editors	Marc Cassini (Text)
	Heather Mills (Research)
Art Directors	Normand Boudreault, Solange Laberge
Designer	Luc Germain, Michel Giguère
Research Editor	Jim McRae
Picture Editor	Christopher Jackson
Writers	Tamsin M. Douglas, Andrew Jones,
	Rob Lutes
Contributing Illustrators	Ronald Durepos, Jean-Pierre
	Bourgeois, Michel Blais, Jacques
	Perrault, Alain Longpré, Jocelyn
	Veillette, Robert Paquet
Administrator	Natalie Watanabe
Production Manager	Michelle Turbide
System Coordinator	Jean-Luc Roy
Photographer	Robert Chartier

Time-Life Books is a division of Time-Life Inc.,
a wholly owned subsidary of
THE TIME INC. BOOK COMPANY

TIME-LIFE BOOKS

President	Mary N. Davis
Publisher	Robert H. Smith
Managing Editor	Thomas H. Flaherty
Director of Editorial Resources	Elise D. Ritter-Clough
Associate Publisher	Trevor Lunn
Marketing Director	Regina Hall
Editorial Director	Donia Ann Steele
Consulting Editor	Bob Doyle, John Sullivan
Production Manager	Marlene Zack

THE CONSULTANTS

John Arno is a consultant, cabinetmaker and freelance writer who lives in Troy, Michigan. He also conducts seminars on wood identification and early American furniture design.

Giles Miller-Mead taught advanced cabinetmaking at Montreal technical schools for more than ten years. A native of New Zealand, he has worked as a restorer of antique furniture.

Andrew Poynter is President of A&M Wood Specialty Inc., of Cambridge, Ontario, Canada, merchants of fine hardwoods and veneers. He began his career in the wood industry in the early '70s making custom furniture. He is now a director of the Woodworkers Alliance for Rainforest Protection and an interim director of the Forest Stewardship Council.

Joseph Truini is Senior Editor of *Home Mechanix* magazine. A former Shop and Tools Editor of *Popular Mechanics*, he has worked as a cabinetmaker, home improvement contractor and carpenter.

Encyclopedia of Wood
    p. cm.—(The Art of Woodworking)
Includes index.
ISBN 0-8094-9916-9. (trade)
ISBN 0-8094-9917-7 (lib)
1. Woodwork--Encyclopedias.
2. Wood--Encyclopedias.
I. Time- Life Books. II. Series
TT180.E613 1992
684' .08—dc20   92-37293
                                        CIP

For information about any Time-Life book, please call 1-800-621-7026, or write:
Reader Information
Time-Life Customer Service
P.O. Box C-32068
Richmond, Virginia
23261-2068

CONTENTS

John Sharp talks about

WOOD IDENTIFICATION

I was exposed to wood identification at an early age while working at our family sawmill in Union County, Tennessee, during the summers. I felt a great deal of curiosity about the vast differences I could see between the logs of various species as they were "opened up" and the lumber moved from the saw deck.

Oak, poplar and other common hardwood logs made up the majority of logs delivered to the mill, but there was the occasional odd species, such as persimmon or sassafras. My job was to separate the lumber by species. If a poplar board was found in a stack of oak, that was my fault, so I quickly learned my woods.

At that time I only knew the common names of the different species. Not until I encountered wood anatomy courses in forestry school did I realize the importance of scientific names, for common names were variable from region to region.

Wood identification has come a long way since the turn of the century, when Yale was the only school teaching forestry studies. Now there are 25 to 30 places where wood identification is offered as part of the curriculum. When I was in forestry school in North Carolina, just after World War II, an integral part of our work involved identifying wood samples. When we came across an unfamiliar species, say sourwood, which wasn't a commercial wood, our task became more difficult. I can still remember a classmate of mine, a war veteran who survived Guadalcanal, remarking that he swore he'd never worry about another thing in his life, but there he was worrying, as we all did, because he couldn't tell the difference between ash and hickory.

At the time, wood identification tools consisted of a hand lens and textbooks featuring small black-and-white photos of species samples. With a view to reducing the anxiety associated with identifying wood, I have worked very closely over the years with a photography lab at the University of Tennessee to get better photos. Wood lovers can now refer to good quality 8-by-10-inch photos of wood types in all sorts of places—from woodworking publications to bookstores in our national parks.

John Sharp is a retired University of Tennessee professor of forestry and a member of the International Wood Collectors Society. He works from his home near Knoxville, Tennessee.

Andrew Poynter talks about
BUYING AND SELLING WOOD

As a supplier of hardwoods and fine veneers for the last 20 years, I have been privileged to get to know some of the finest woodworkers in North America. I've also learned a lot about wood and its qualities, not only the good qualities, but the baffling ones as well.

Looking back, I suppose my own interest in wood began many years before I established my company. In fact, I can vividly recall my first hands-on experience with a piece of Brazilian rosewood—completely captivating!

That was in the mid-'60s, and in those days wood turners, luthiers and furniture-makers had little to choose from in the way of different woods. Although they could read wonderful descriptive passages about Macassar ebony, satinwood, kingwood, and so on, trying to find a reliable source for all those fine woods was next to impossible. The need to inventory a selection of wood for the furniture that I pictured myself making was one of the reasons I started my wood dealership in 1973.

My furnituremaking gradually tapered off, and by 1975 I was putting all my efforts into the task of marketing and selling fine hardwoods and veneers. At that time, everyone said the rain forests would go on forever, and that there was so much wood in the Amazon that we would never run out. However, the passage of time and the demand for wood have done two things to the timber trade: First, a proliferation of wood dealers and wood varieties have entered the marketplace—a plus for those of us who love wood. Second, we became complacent about the true value of various species and the sustainability of their supply. We are now only too aware that the rain forests may not go on forever.

Although the problems causing deforestation are very complex, there are steps that woodworkers should take to help improve the situation. "Measure twice and cut once" may seem almost too basic, but it can make a difference in reducing our consumption. Using veneer whenever possible is another step in the right direction.

I've become an active member of the Woodworkers Alliance for Rainforest Protection. WARP was founded in 1989 by a concerned group of woodworkers, wood turners, luthiers, wood merchants, tool dealers and lovers of wood. Central to many of its programs, WARP encourages the use of wood from sustainable or well-managed sources. It is now evident that much has to change in global forestry practices over the next few years if woodworkers in the future are to enjoy the remarkable selection of wood that is available to all of us today.

Andrew Poynter holds a piece of redwood burl at his store, A & M Wood Specialty Inc., in Cambridge, Ontario. The company sells more than 100 types of wood to woodworkers throughout North America.

Jon Arno talks about some
FAVORITE WOODS

Since I grew up in a family that owned a lumber business, working with wood has been a lifelong interest of mine. While many fellow woodworkers tend to concentrate on tools and methods of construction, I find that the real essence of the craft lies in the medium we use—the wood itself. The world provides a great many fine timbers and some of them, such as walnut, mahogany and rosewood, lend a certain prestige to the finished project. For me, the joy of woodworking comes from discovering the special properties of various species and learning how to choose the most functional wood for the intended purpose, regardless of its notoriety or reputation. Every wood has an application for which it is unsurpassed. The goal of good craftsmanship is to discover just what that application is.

There are literally hundreds of woods, some of them reasonably plentiful domestic species, that seldom find their way into lumberyards. Nevertheless, they are still outstanding woods for certain applications. A few of my favorites are catalpa, balsam poplar and black ash. Recently, I have added another one to my list—sassafras.

A member of the Laurel family—along with cinnamon, camphor and bay—sassafras is well known for its sweet-scented oil used in cosmetics and soaps. Its buoyant, decay-resistant wood has also gained some popularity with boat builders. Cabinetmakers, however, have long dismissed sassafras as being too soft and brittle. Basically, these assessments are accurate; the challenge for me has been to find an application where this wood excels. Oddly enough, the answer has come from what many perceive as one of its negative qualities.

Sassafras is brittle, but its resistance to flexing gives it outstanding resonance when used as the soundboard in dulcimers. The bright, bell-like tone it yields is as pleasant as the spicy aroma of the wood when it is being cut, shaped and sanded. And what role could be more fitting for this uniquely American species than in helping to provide the voice for an American musical instrument?

I started making dulcimers only a couple of years ago, when my daughter, a music lover, chose to build one for a high school project. We bought a kit, but when I opened the box I realized that there wasn't anything inside that I couldn't make in my own shop, so I started to experiment. My only regret, so far as being a luthier, is I don't possess a sense of music to go along with it.

Jon Arno displays a home-made dulcimer, fashioned from sassafras and osage orange. He is a wood technologist, consultant and freelance writer living in Troy, Michigan.

UNDERSTANDING WOOD

A pile of logs sit at a sawmill in Oregon, ready to be milled into lumber.

As you strive to improve your mastery of the demanding craft of woodworking, much of your attention will be devoted to learning about tools and the techniques for using them. But in your quest for perfection, do not neglect the most fundamental component of every project—the wood itself.

Rarely perfect and always varying, each piece of wood exhibits its own character, just as certainly as a human being: Some woods are plain, some colorful; some are stable, some unpredictable; some work easily, some with difficulty. A knowledge of these properties will allow you to make the most of your abilities, achieving a wedding of form, substance and technique that can transform even an ordinary project into a work of art.

You can obtain much factual information about the properties of wood in readily available books and articles. Learning to apply that knowledge is more challenging. For example, the knowledge that maple boards may contain wide variations in color, texture and figure will assume greater meaning as you learn to use these characteristics to best advantage. Likewise, although Douglas-fir is an attractive, easily worked wood, variations in its surface porosity can make it difficult to finish well. But when you learn how to seal the wood, you will find many uses for Douglas-fir. Experience will also tell you that a resilient wood such as pine is more forgiving of less precise joinery, while dense, brittle species such as mahogany demand joints that are cut to close tolerances. And every beginner quickly learns that sanding wood across the grain, rather than parallel to it, results in scratches that are accentuated when a finish is applied to the piece.

Remember, too, that how a particular piece of wood behaves in your shop depends in large measure on what happened to it before it reached the lumberyard. How the wood grew in the tree, the weather the tree endured and how the wood was cut and dried all affect the final product. The wood of a leaning tree, for example, will react differently during machining than that sawn from the trunk of an erect tree. And whether a board is quartersawn or plain-sawn has an impact on its dimensional stability.

One way to obtain intimate knowledge of your material is to saw it yourself from a tree using a portable lumber mill *(page 36)*. Selecting and felling a tree, bucking—or crosscutting—it into logs, and milling the planks impart a hands-on understanding that is impossible to acquire any other way. The work is arduous, and it also takes considerable time to cut and dry the boards. But the rewards—both in the unique lumber produced and the personal satisfaction in producing it—are well worth the effort.

A stand of Douglas-fir trees basks in the sunlight in a West Coast forest. Many softwoods, like Douglas-fir, are ideal for interior trim or cabinet work.

ANATOMY OF A TREE

Harvested from the trunks and branches of trees, wood is a resilient, dynamic building material. Understanding how trees grow can shed considerable light on why wood behaves as it does when it is worked or finished.

All trees consist of three major systems: a root network that draws water and minerals from the soil; a crown of leaves, where water and minerals are combined with carbon dioxide in the presence of sunlight to produce food for the tree (photosynthesis); and—of most interest to woodworkers—a supporting trunk that transports the water and food.

Viewed in cross section, a tree trunk at first appears to be a fairly homogenous column of wood, marked by a series of concentric bands called growth rings. However, a close view reveals a series of distinct layers wrapped around each other, some living, some not. At the center is the heartwood, the densest—and dead—part of the trunk. Encircling the heartwood is the paler sapwood, which in turn is surrounded by the cambium, the trunk's only actively growing segment. The cambium's growth accounts for the layers of sapwood that are added each year. On either side of the cambium are layers that transport sap throughout the tree and store surplus food. As the inner sapwood recedes from the cambium, its pores gradually clog with resins and gums, and become heartwood. As the outer sections become dormant, they form a trunk's outermost layer, the bark.

The differences between sapwood and heartwood are important to every woodworker. Because it is more porous than heartwood, sapwood absorbs finishes better. But the denser heartwood is usually more durable and decay-resistant. The carbohydrates present in sapwood cells make the wood vulnerable to fungi and insects. The colors of heartwood are also generally richer and more vibrant than those of sapwood.

Crown
The branches and leaves of a tree, where photosynthesis takes place

Trunk
Also called stem or bole; supports tree and channels nutrients to and from roots

Roots
Anchor tree and absorb water and minerals from the soil

Growth rings

In regions where a tree's growth is interrupted by seasonal change, its wood is characterized by growth rings: concentric bands, usually fractions of an inch wide, perpendicular to the axis of the trunk. Trees that grow in temperate areas with a winter season display distinct rings. In the tropics, where growth is more or less continuous, a sharply defined ring may only be visible as the result of a dry season. The rings are intersected by a series of rays: flattened bands of tissue that radiate outward from the pith to the phloem of the tree. Growth rings consist of two separate layers. The first, called earlywood, is laid down at the beginning of the growing season; the second layer, or late-wood, is formed toward the end. Earlywood is more porous than latewood, which accounts for the contrast between the two. Taken together, the earlywood and latewood of a growth ring in temperate climates represent one year in a tree's life. The width of a ring depends on growing conditions and varies from species to species, but changes from year to year reveal a tree's history. A wide ring suggests a growing season with ample sun and moisture, while a narrow ring is evidence of disease, unfavorable weather or insect attacks. For the woodworker, growth rings are also clues to the strength of the wood: uncharacteristically narrow or wide rings can signal weak timber.

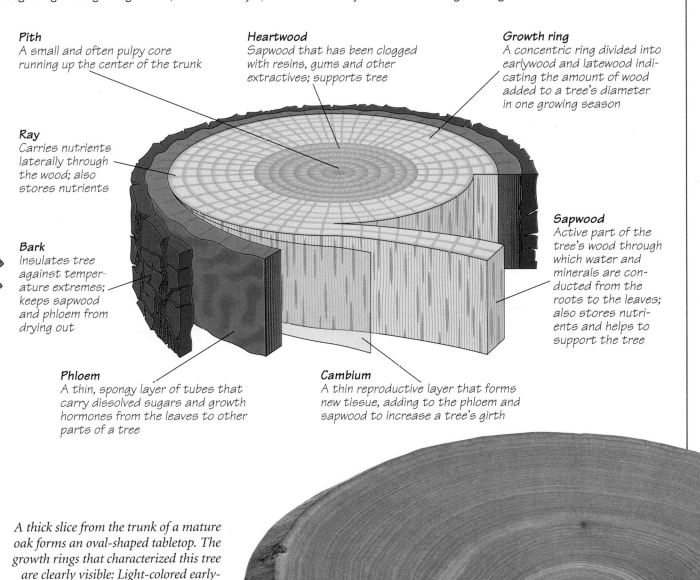

Pith
A small and often pulpy core running up the center of the trunk

Heartwood
Sapwood that has been clogged with resins, gums and other extractives; supports tree

Growth ring
A concentric ring divided into earlywood and latewood indicating the amount of wood added to a tree's diameter in one growing season

Ray
Carries nutrients laterally through the wood; also stores nutrients

Bark
Insulates tree against temperature extremes; keeps sapwood and phloem from drying out

Sapwood
Active part of the tree's wood through which water and minerals are conducted from the roots to the leaves; also stores nutrients and helps to support the tree

Phloem
A thin, spongy layer of tubes that carry dissolved sugars and growth hormones from the leaves to other parts of a tree

Cambium
A thin reproductive layer that forms new tissue, adding to the phloem and sapwood to increase a tree's girth

A thick slice from the trunk of a mature oak forms an oval-shaped tabletop. The growth rings that characterized this tree are clearly visible: Light-colored early-wood alternates with darker bands of latewood, etching a distinct line between each year's growing periods.

SOFTWOODS AND HARDWOODS

Trees are roughly divided into softwoods and hardwoods, but the terms are inexact: Some hardwoods, such as basswood or aspen, for example, are softer than North American softwoods like longleaf pine or Douglas-fir.

The type and shape of a tree's leaves are more accurate indicators of a particular wood's identity. Softwoods include evergreen conifers with needle-like leaves, while hardwoods comprise broad-leaved deciduous, or leaf-shedding, trees. But it is at the microscopic level that the true differences between softwoods and hardwoods can be seen. Softwoods are composed mainly of tracheids, dual-purpose cells which conduct the sap up through the trunk and provide support. Hardwoods, which are believed to have evolved later, have narrower, thicker-walled fiber cells for support and large-diameter thin-walled vessels for sap conduction. These cells determine the texture of a tree's wood.

In spring, when there is abundant moisture and rapid growth of earlywood, the tracheid cells in softwoods have thin walls and large cavities to conduct the sap. The result is relatively porous wood. As latewood develops in the latter part of the growing season, the tracheids begin to form thicker walls, creating denser wood.

In hardwoods such as oak or ash, most of the vessels develop in the earlywood, resulting in uneven grain. These species are called ring-porous. With diffuse-porous hardwoods such as maple, the vessels are distributed more evenly in the earlywood and latewood. Some species, such as walnut, exhibit a more gradual transition from earlywood to latewood and are termed semi-ring-porous or semi-diffuse-porous.

The differences in cell structure between softwoods and hardwoods become apparent when a stain is applied. In softwoods, the light, porous earlywood absorbs stain more readily than the dark, denser latewood—in effect reversing the grain pattern like a photographic negative. Hardwoods, however, absorb stain more evenly, enhancing the grain pattern.

CELL STRUCTURE OF SOFTWOODS AND HARDWOODS

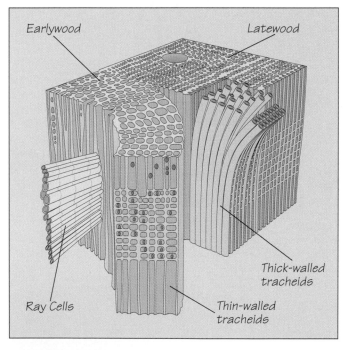
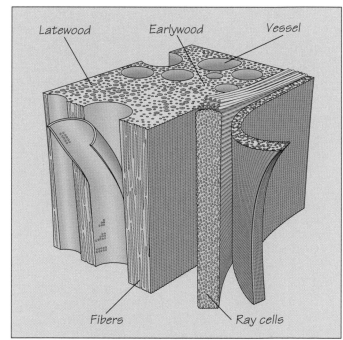

A microscopic view
The differences between softwood and hardwood are readily apparent when viewed under a microscope's magnification. The cell structure of softwoods *(above, left)* is much simpler than that of hardwoods. Almost all softwood cells are long, thin tracheids, which support an unbroken column of sap that can tower more than 200 feet. The tracheids in latewood become thicker-walled than those in earlywood. In hardwoods *(above, right)*, the sap is conducted through vessels, a series of tubelike cells stacked one atop the other. Support for the trunk is provided by fiber cells. In the ring-porous hardwood shown, vessels are more prominent in earlywood; fibers are the predominant cell type in latewood. In both hardwoods and softwoods, storage cells for carbohydrates and starch make up the remaining non-vascular wood tissue.

A ROSEWOOD BY ANY OTHER NAME...

For the practicing woodworker, calling a piece of wood by its common name seldom creates confusion. If you ask for a few planks of white oak at a lumber yard, for example, there is no reason why you should not get what you requested. But with some species, particularly exotics that must be purchased by mail-order, identities can be less certain. Common names are misleading when trees with different characteristics share the same name, or when the same species has different common names in separate localities.

Suppose you wanted samples of a very rare and expensive species like Brazilian rosewood, a black-streaked, dark brown wood often used in the making of superior-quality guitars. A supplier could in good conscience send you pieces of kingwood or tulip-wood instead, since both belong to the rosewood family and are native to Brazil. In fact, there are several genuine rosewoods, such as East Indian rosewood and cocobolo, that cost much less than the Brazilian variety and are easier to find. However, they might not fit the bill for a guitar-maker. Other species, such as bocote, bubinga and padauk, are often sold as rosewood substitutes, but do not look at all like Brazilian rosewood.

To avoid confusion, it is helpful to refer to certain woods by their botanical names. Brazilian rosewood is *Dalbergia nigra*, and a guitar-maker who requests it by that name will not be disappointed.

This scientific naming system was developed more than 200 years ago by Swedish botanist Carl Linnaeus.

As shown below, in a botanical analysis of Brazilian rosewood, Linnaeus' now universally accepted scheme classifies plants into the various taxonomic groups of phyla, classes, orders, families, genera and species. Almost all trees belong to the spermatophyta phylum, with hardwoods in the angiospermae sub-phylum and the dicotyledonae class, and softwoods belonging to the gymnospermae subphylum.

**A botanical breakdown
of Brazilian rosewood**
Phylum: *Spermatophyta*
Sub-phylum: *Angiospermae*
Class: *Dicotyledonae*
Order: *Rosales*
Family: *Leguminosae*
Genus: *Dalbergia*
Species: *Nigra*

THE HIDDEN HARVEST

In addition to lumber and manufactured boards, trees provide a cornucopia of raw materials for products such as rolls of newsprint (left). For centuries, people have extracted such natural products as cork, rubber, gum, medicine, spices, drugs, oils, charcoal, camphor and resins. The cellulose fiber found in trees is used in the production of plastics and lacquers as well as wood pulp. Coniferous trees supply turpentine and resins, which are used in paints, inks and finishes. Modern chemistry has unlocked still more of wood's hidden treasures, finding ways to remove such disparate products as glues, poisons and artificial vanilla.

FROM LOG TO LUMBER

Between the standing tree and the boards you pick off the rack at the lumberyard stands a complex process that requires many people to apply enormous skill at every step. Undetected defects in the standing tree, damage caused during felling, poor judgment in bucking or inattentive sawing at the mill can sabotage the value of a tree and raise the sawmill's—and the wood-buying consumer's—costs. Although power saws have replaced muscle-driven pit saws in the forest and at the mill, and cuts are now guided by laser beams and computer technology instead of chalk lines, no replacement has been devised for the practiced eye of an experienced lumberman.

A tractor-like skidder hauls a hitch of logs from the forest.

A logger (left) makes his undercut in a mighty Douglas-fir tree in the rain forests of British Columbia, Canada. Felling these behemoths was once the work of two men pushing and pulling a huge felling saw; today, a chain saw reduces felling to a quick one-man job.

A hydraulic log loader dispenses its contents onto a truck.

Selecting the trees

A tree's journey to the lumberyard begins in the woods, when a forester or timber cruiser evaluates the trees for cutting. Not all cut trees will be earmarked for the saw mill; some will be used for pulp or firewood. These lower-grade trees are deliberately harvested to give the residual stock better access to nutrients and more room to grow, thus increasing the timber stand's value. The very best trees will be reserved for veneer.

Since most of the highest-grade lumber will come from the area just under the bark, the forester must be able to detect at a glance clues that betray defects in this area. Knots, for example, can be particularly troublesome, depending on where they are located. In the bottom part of the tree, where they are usually indicated by a slight disfiguration of the bark, knots may be so deeply overgrown that they will not affect the value of the outer wood. But further up, where they are typically indicated by concentric circles or even bumps in the bark, knots pose more serious problems in terms of quality.

The ability to distinguish between different types of fungi is another important skill in tree evaluation. All fungi cause some damage, but certain species are rapacious: In beech and hard maple, for example, a single body of false tinder fungus on the outside of a tree may signal the presence of a 12- to 14-foot-long column of decay within. If the decay were confined to the center of the tree, this would be less of a problem, but many fungi infest the most valuable outer wood. Any scarring of the bark is thus suspicious, since even the tiniest opening makes a tree susceptible to fungal infection.

Bird damage—specifically peckholes made by the yellow-bellied sapsucker—also affects a tree's commercial value. Unlike its woodpecker cousins, which eat wood-boring insects that infest dead wood, the yellow-bellied sapsucker feasts on the sap, wood cells, and inner bark of live trees. Persistent feeding results in long streaks of stain that effectively render the wood worthless.

Felling and bucking

Trees are cut with three passes of a chain saw. The first two cuts remove a wedge about one-third of the diameter of the tree, facing the intended direction of fall. The tree is felled by the third cut, or backcut, made opposite to and a few inches above the wedge. As the tree falls, its direction is controlled by a "hinge"

of wood between the wedge and backcut. Expert fellers consider many factors before making the cuts—the condition of the felling site, wind direction, the lean of the tree, and the presence of dead branches in adjacent trees, aptly called "widowmakers."

Once the limbs have been removed, the tree is skidded to a staging area, or landing, where it is bucked into logs. To ensure that the wood is cut to the highest possible grade, the bucker—like the forester or tree cruiser beforehand—has to "read" the tree for signs of defects before setting to work. Bulges in the bark indicate knots that are close to the sur-

face; large-diameter rotting branches point to decay within the tree trunk. While the optimal length for hardwood logs is 16 feet (8 feet for veneer-quality logs), cutting logs to this length is not always possible. Sometimes the bucker cuts 8-foot and 12-foot logs to avoid defects that would render a larger log worthless.

Transporting the logs

In some parts of North America, especially the Pacific Northwest where trees are exceptionally large, bucking is done at the felling site before the logs are transported to a central yard. Steeply sloping

Although a variety of methods have been used to move logs to the lumber mill, from river runs to draft horses, trucking remains the most common method of transport in North America.

The narrow kerf of a band saw produces less waste than a circular saw. Here, a worker at a Vermont mill removes a 38-foot-long band saw blade for sharpening.

terrain may require the logs to be gathered in from the forest floor using a series of cables. One such system is known as high-lead logging. Two main cables—one called a haulback and the other a mainline—are rigged to the top of a tall mast. Several other cables, called chokers, dangle from the mainline. Trees are felled so they land with their butt sections pointing uphill; crewmen wrap each choker around the butt section of a bucked-up log, signal the head operator, and the logs are reeled up the hill to the central pile, usually located next to a lumber road. When the logs have been detached, the haulback cable is used to pull the mainline and its chokers for another load. No matter how they are moved from the felling site or when they

are bucked, logs are loaded onto trucks with a hydraulic grapple hook for the trip to the sawmill.

In the sawmill

There are two main types of sawmills: those that use a band saw, and those that use a circular saw. A sawmill is often described according to the type of wood it cuts and the type of saw it employs, such as a softwood band mill or a hardwood circular mill. Large band mills are often required for the larger-sized logs that are common in the softwood industry in western North America. Circular sawmills, more common in smaller hardwood operations in the East, have a smaller capacity, but are far less expensive than band mills.

The sawing process generates a great deal of "waste"—almost one-third of the bulk of each log—but every possible bit of wood is chipped up and used. Some is sold to paper pulp mills or wood-fired utilities. (The volume of wood-burned fuel has increased substantially since the energy crunch of the early 1970s. Today wood supplies about 3 percent of the United States' energy consumption.) Even the bark, which is immediately stripped off the logs, frequently powers the sawmill's drying kilns.

The bark is stripped from the log with large grinding cutterheads or blasted off by high-pressure water jets. The log is then mounted on a log carriage, positioned so that the first cuts slice off the widest, clearest, most valuable boards.

In less than 2 seconds, this band saw blade, driven by a 150-horsepower engine, can slice through a 16-foot log. The red line—a laser beam—shows the operator where the blade will cut.

In the mill, the sawyer may rotate the log to "read" the log's hidden defects. While in the past this might have been done by hand, it is not uncommon to see today's sawyers work in a glass-enclosed booth, forming judgments with the help of advanced electronic equipment. In such a mill, the sawyer uses joysticks—like those of a computer game—to twirl the log almost a full turn in a matter of seconds, firing a beam of laser light down its length to visualize the effect of a particular cut before it is made. In the most efficient mills, sophisticated computers are used to select the best position to obtain the maximum production from each log.

First, the four outer slabs of the log are removed, giving the sawyer a clean plane from which to make his next cut—the so-called "opening face"—to give the widest, clearest board available. Once this face is cut, the log is rotated, and three additional boards are cut— one from each remaining face. Large mills handling big logs send the remain-ing square timber—called a cant—to a resawing area for cutting into various sizes of dimension lumber. Here again, this sawyer must determine the optimum cutting pattern that will yield the most valuable lumber. All the boards are edged, trimmed to length and graded.

Smaller mills, and those handling smaller logs, may use a different sawing strategy. After removing the outer slabs, the boards are cut from the opening face until defects interfere. Then the log is rotated to the next clearest face. As with the first method, the remaining cant is resawn into lower grade lumber. Finally, the boards are sorted, stacked and stickered—separated by thin strips to allow air to circulate between them—for their trip to the drying kiln, where they will remain for up to 50 days.

A device known as a "slot machine" sorts freshly sawn boards into the right widths and lengths.

LUMBER CUTTING METHODS

Converting a log into lumber requires certain compromises. Most logs are sawn in one of three basic ways. The simplest method squares the log and slices it into boards straight through from one side to the other. This technique, known as through-and-through sawing, results in stock cut tangentially to the annual growth rings. A second method, plain-sawing, is similar, except that the log is rotated as it is cut, and the low-quality pith is set aside for items such as pallets. Plain-sawn lumber is also known as flat-grained lumber.

The growth rings in this quartersawn oak board appear as lines that are parallel to the board's edges.

The third method, called quarter-sawing or edge-grain sawing, divides the log into four quarters and cuts every board more or less radially. Quarter-sawn boards have their annual growth rings perpendicular to the face.

This orientation of the growth rings accounts for the dimensional stability of quartersawn boards. Wood shrinks and expands roughly twice as much tangentially to the rings as its does radially. When quartersawn boards swell or shrink they do so mostly in thickness, which is minimal, whereas a plain-sawn board changes across its width. A dining table made from plain-sawn pine boards, for example, can change as much as 1 inch in width; a similar table made from quartersawn boards would only swell or shrink by one-third as much.

THREE METHODS OF SAWING LOGS

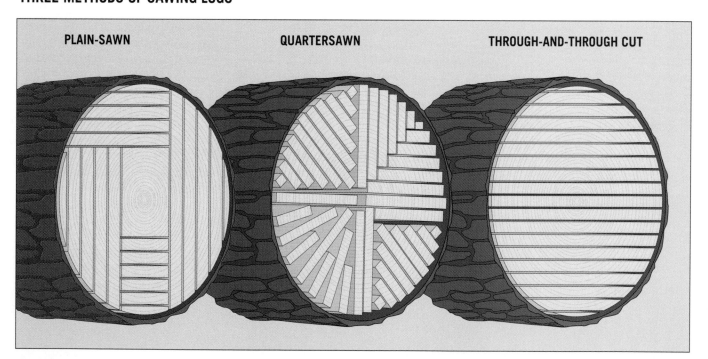

| PLAIN-SAWN | QUARTERSAWN | THROUGH-AND-THROUGH CUT |

Choosing the best method

Cutting logs into lumber at a sawmill is a balance between intended use, structural stability and esthetic appearance. Plain-sawing *(above, left)* produces boards of diminishing width as the log is rotated to make successive cuts. The more expensive method, called quartersawing *(above, center)*, limits board width to the radius of the log. But it produces more dimensionally stable lumber, making it ideal for drawer sides, tabletops and frame rails. Through-and-through sawing *(above, right)* yields the maximum number of usable boards from a log; the outer boards are plain-sawn, while the inner boards are quartersawn.

Quartersawing also offers an esthetic advantage: It exposes the medullary rays that radiate from the heart of a log like the spokes of a wheel. In most species the rays are only one cell thick, but in a few species, such as oak, the ray cells are thicker and appear as vivid streaks scattered along the grain. Sycamore, poplar and basswood are also ideal candidates for quartersawing.

As the illustration at the bottom of page 24 shows, quartersawn lumber is not always cut perpendicular to the grain, and some through-and-through cut boards close to the center of a log will have quartersawn grain. Therefore, no matter how they are actually cut, boards with growth rings at angles between 45° and 90° to the wide surface are classified quartersawn, while boards

with rings at 0° to 45° angles to the wide surface are termed plain-sawn. Boards with growth rings at a 30° to 60° angle are also called rift-sawn or bastard-sawn.

In actual practice, sawyers use a myriad of sawing patterns, depending on the type of machinery being used, the intended use of the lumber, log diameter and the type of tree. For example, in virtually all trees the pith or central core of the heartwood is less desirable than and not as strong as the rest of the heartwood. Plain-sawing "boxes out the heart" by cutting around it to eliminate it.

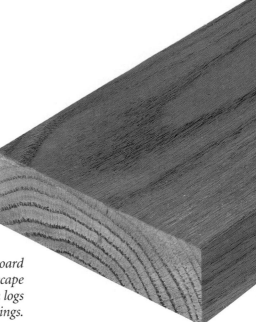

The growth rings in this plain-sawn oak board appear on the face as an elliptical landscape figure. Plain-sawn stock is sliced from logs with most of the cuts tangent to the rings.

ADVANTAGES OF PLAIN-SAWN AND QUARTERSAWN LUMBER

PLAIN-SAWN	QUARTERSAWN
Cheaper and easier to obtain	More dimensionally stable
Shrinks and swells less in thickness	Shrinks and swells less across the board
Usually comes in greater variety of widths	Twists and cups less
Less susceptible to collapse during drying; easier to kiln dry	Splits and checks less in seasoning and in use
Figure patterns resulting from the difference between earlywood and latewood in the growth rings are more conspicuous	Raised grain caused by the swelling of the earlywood in growth rings not as pronounced
Has more interesting figure	Figure due to pronounced rays more conspicuous
Round or oval knots that may occur have less effect on structural integrity	Holds finishes better in some species
Pockets of pitch extend through fewer boards	Sapwood in boards appears at the edges and is easily cut off
Not as susceptible to splitting when nails or screws driven through face	Wears more evenly

PROPERTIES OF WOOD

An experienced woodworker pays close attention to the selection of wood for a project. Every species has unique qualities that can make it ideal for one application but unsuitable for another. Among the key properties that distinguish woods are color, grain, texture, figure, weight and odor.

Many species are prized for their distinctive colors. Padauk is a fiery orange-red; black walnut often exhibits deep purples and chocolate tones. Color in wood is the result of extractives such as tannins, gums and resins in the wood. When cut lumber is exposed to air, these substances gradually oxidize, deepening the wood's color. In some cases, however, the color may fade.

Grain and texture are two distinct properties that are often confused. Grain describes the direction and regularity of the wood fibers relative to the axis of the tree trunk. As illustrated on page 28, the grain displayed by a piece of lumber depends on the growth pattern of the tree from which it was cut.

A wood's texture depends on the size and distribution of its cells. Ring-porous hardwoods with large vessels have a coarse texture, while diffuse-porous hardwoods with fine vessels have a finer texture. In some softwoods, abrupt transitions from earlywood to latewood produce an uneven texture. Where there is little or no transition, as in white pine, the wood has an even texture.

Landscape figure on white birch

Fiddleback figure on peroba rosa

Mottle figure on movingue

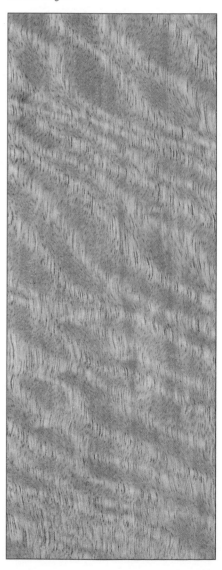

Figure—an important quality in veneers—is the pattern displayed on the surface of a board. This is the expression of a board's "character"—the sum of its grain, contrast between earlywood and latewood, eccentricity of growth rings, mineral streaks, disease and the method used to saw the log. Some of the more stunning figures in different species are illustrated below. For example, plain-sawn white birch reveals a so-called landscape figure. Interlocked grain produces the rib-bon figure common in African mahogany. Wavy grain in maples results in a fiddle-back figure, so named because of its use in the backs of violins. And irregular growths on the outer surfaces of trees, such as elm, yield an intricate burl figure.

The weight of different wood species is expressed as specific gravity, or its den-sity compared to an equal volume of water. The specific gravity of an oven-dried sample of American elm, for example, is 0.50, making it half as heavy as a tropical hardwood like ekki, which has the same specific gravity as water—1.00. Lignum vitae, the heaviest wood, has a specific gravity of 1.23. The high-er a wood's specific gravity, the less porous it is and the more impervious it will be to a finish.

A wood's odor—usually caused by oils in the heartwood—may also deter-mine its use. An aromatic species like cedar, for example, is often used for clothes chests and cigar boxes.

Ribbon figure
on African mahogany

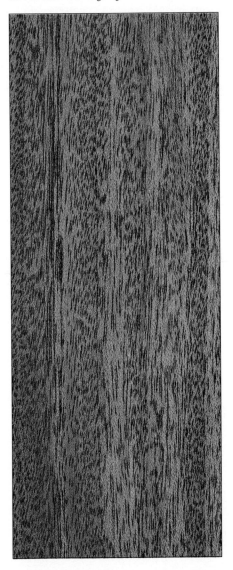

Bird's-eye figure
on maple

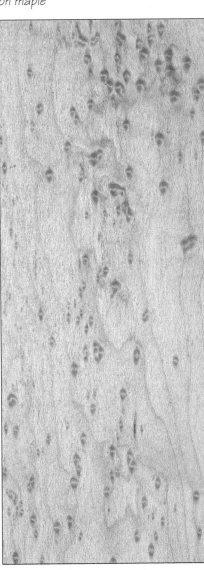

Burl figure
on Carpathian elm

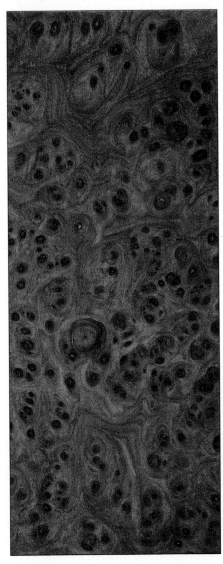

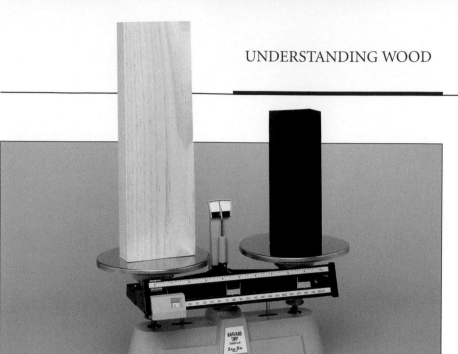

Specific gravity is a better indicator of a wood's weight than size. With a specific gravity of 0.90, a piece of ebony weighs the same as a much larger block of white pine, whose specific gravity is only 0.35.

TYPES OF GRAIN

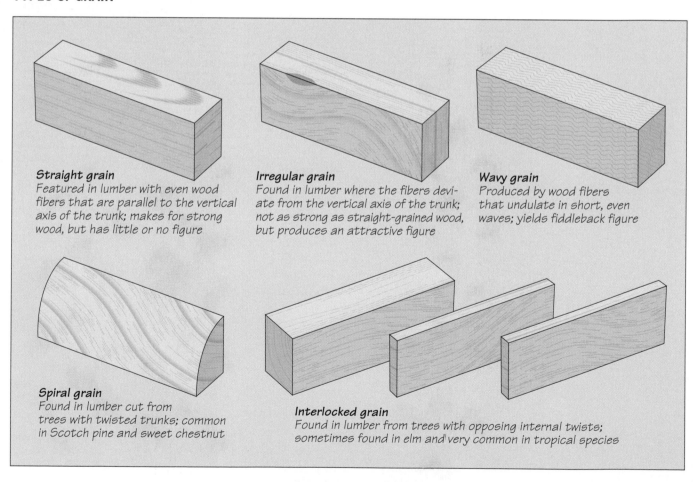

Straight grain
Featured in lumber with even wood fibers that are parallel to the vertical axis of the trunk; makes for strong wood, but has little or no figure

Irregular grain
Found in lumber where the fibers deviate from the vertical axis of the trunk; not as strong as straight-grained wood, but produces an attractive figure

Wavy grain
Produced by wood fibers that undulate in short, even waves; yields fiddleback figure

Spiral grain
Found in lumber cut from trees with twisted trunks; common in Scotch pine and sweet chestnut

Interlocked grain
Found in lumber from trees with opposing internal twists; sometimes found in elm and very common in tropical species

WORKING WITH THE GRAIN

Reading the grain

Many woodworking tasks, especially planing, require working in the direction of the grain. You can usually tell grain orientation by running your hand along a board face: The surface will feel smoother when your hand is moving with the grain and rougher when running against it. Another method is to slide a smoothing plane lightly along the face in one direction, then repeat in the opposite direction. The blade will chatter or catch on the wood fibers when it is cutting against the grain. As shown on the plain-sawn board at right, the wood fibers slope "uphill" in the direction of the grain and "downhill" against it.

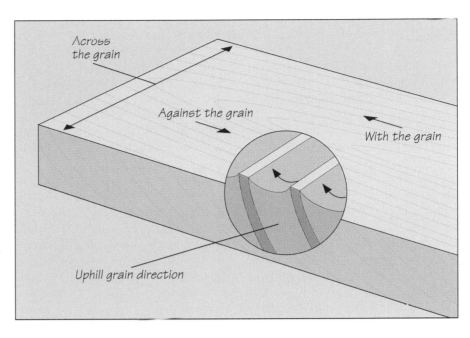

Across the grain

Against the grain

With the grain

Uphill grain direction

Determining the best direction to plane

To prevent a plane blade from catching the grain and tearing or chipping the wood fibers, always cut in the uphill grain direction. This will produce clean shavings and a smooth surface. Be especially careful to spot grain that changes direction within a single board. The diagram at left shows several typical grain patterns with arrows indicating the best planing direction. The uphill direction may be constant from one end of a board to the other (A). Or it may change, demanding that you plane from each end toward the middle (B). It could also change from the middle to the ends (C). If the grain does not slope at all, you can plane in a single pass from either end (D).

A

B

C

D

IDENTIFYING WOOD

Whether you are restoring a piece of furniture made from an unfamiliar wood or debating the authenticity of a particular board with a local lumberyard, a knack for identifying a piece of lumber is a useful skill.

Of course, an entire branch of knowledge is devoted to wood science and technology. Books have been written about the subject, careers have been founded upon it, and universities offer courses and degrees devoted to it. Scientists identify wood by first slicing off a thin sliver of a sample, then mounting it on a slide and examining it under a microscope.

The practicing woodworker, however, who is more interested in sawing than in science, can successfully identify most woods by methodically searching for a few simple clues with the help of inexpensive equipment. Most of the tools you need are illustrated at right. Your investigation should begin with the easily observable properties of the sample (*page 26*). Examine and feel the surface; determine whether it is oily or dry, dull or lustrous. Check its hardness by trying to dent the surface with a fingernail. You

may be able to tell with the naked eye whether a hardwood is ring- or diffuse-porous. As shown in the photos on page 33, these two types of hardwood are relatively easy to tell apart when viewed with a hand lens. Note whether the texture of the wood is coarse or smooth. If the sample has been recently cut, it may have a recognizable odor. If it has been sufficiently dried, you may be able to calculate its specific gravity.

Although these observations can help narrow down the choices, you will still have to view a wood sample under magnification in order to hazard an educated guess as to its species. The illustration on page 31 shows the three ways that a sample can be studied: transversely, radially or tangentially. Each method exposes a different view of a sample's anatomical structure. The simplest view is the transverse since it involves looking at the end grain of the sample. However, to avoid a blurred view of crushed fibers, you must first shave the surface with a razor blade or a well-sharpened knife. To get a tangential view of a sample, you will need to make a clean cut along the growth rings of the wood (*page 32*). Making a second cut at right angles to the first exposes a radial view.

Once you have observed and recorded the sample's properties and microscopic details, you can compare the results with a printed key of wood species to identify the wood.

TOOLS FOR THE WOOD SLEUTH

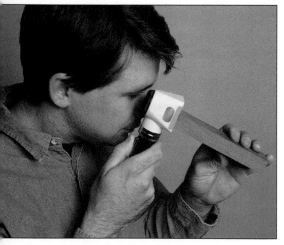

Examining the end grain of a board through an illuminated 10x magnifier enlarges several features of a wood sample that are helpful in species identification.

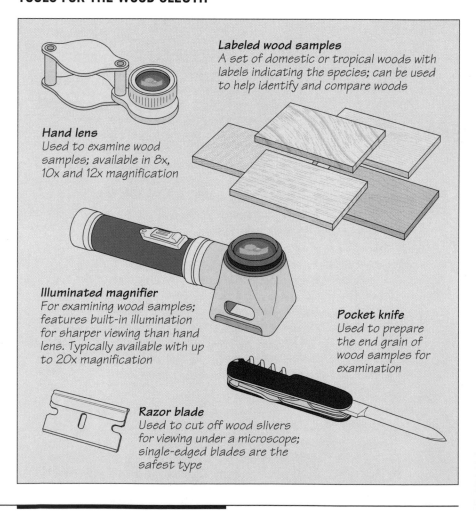

Labeled wood samples
A set of domestic or tropical woods with labels indicating the species; can be used to help identify and compare woods

Hand lens
Used to examine wood samples; available in 8x, 10x and 12x magnification

Illuminated magnifier
For examining wood samples; features built-in illumination for sharper viewing than hand lens. Typically available with up to 20x magnification

Pocket knife
Used to prepare the end grain of wood samples for examination

Razor blade
Used to cut off wood slivers for viewing under a microscope; single-edged blades are the safest type

EXAMINING A WOOD SAMPLE

Three viewing perspectives

The 10x magnification provided by a magnifier or hand lens allows you to examine three views of wood's structure, represented by the hardwood log section shown at right. The transverse section lies at right angles to the grain and is visible in the end grain of stock. The tangential and radial sections are at 90° to the transverse section. The tangential section follows a straight line that is tangent to the growth rings. This section is the surface you see on the face of plain-sawn lumber. A radial section is exposed by cutting a straight line from the bark through the pith, exposing grain lines that appear as vertical strips.

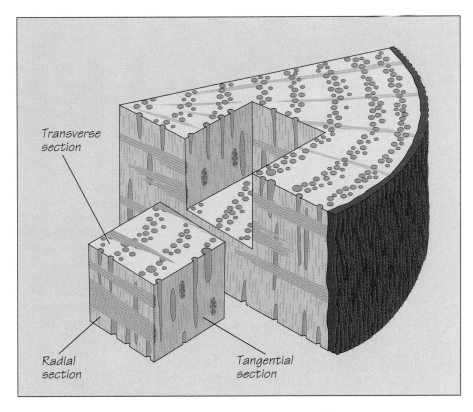

Transverse section

Radial section

Tangential section

| TRANSVERSE SECTION | TANGENTIAL SECTION |

Earlywood   Latewood

Tracheid   Resin canal

Rays

Examining wood under a microscope

At 100x magnification, a microscope uncovers more details of the cellular structure of wood than can be seen through a hand magnifier. At left are two views of white pine, illustrating key elements in species identification. The transverse section *(far left)* shows the size of the tracheid cells and the transition in their density from ear-lywood to latewood. Also evident is a longitudinal resin canal. The tangential section *(near left)* shows the number and thickness of the rays in the wood.

PREPARING WOOD SAMPLES FOR VIEWING WITH A LENS

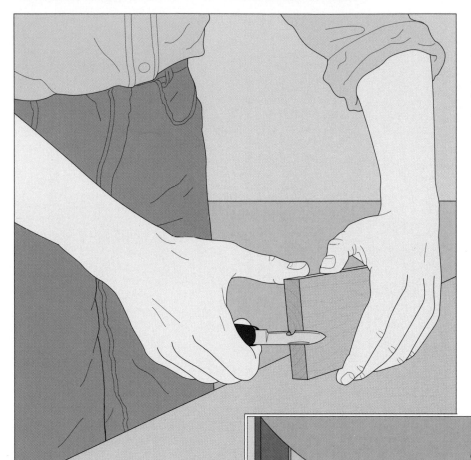

Preparing a transverse section
Slice off a sliver of wood from the end grain of your sample using a sharp knife or razor blade *(left)*. The surface should be smooth and even. If the wood is particularly dense and difficult to cut, first soak the end grain for a short time in hot water.

Tangential cut

Radial cut

Cutting tangential and radial sections
For a tangential section, mark a cutting line tangent to the growth rings on the edge of the sample. Cut along the line with a band saw, making sure your hands are not in line with the blade of the tool *(right)*. For a radial section, make an end-to-end cut through the sample at the high point of the growth rings with the piece face down on the band saw table. To clean up the cuts for viewing, lightly smooth the surfaces with a hand plane. Avoid using sandpaper, which will crush the fibers.

WOOD IDENTIFICATION METHODS

Although identifying wood requires careful observation of the appropriate features of a sample, practice makes the job easier. First measure the width of the growth rings, and note the color and luster of the wood. Remember that wood exposed to sunlight and air changes color, so the hue of a freshly cut sample may be different after it has dried. Luster is not a common feature of many woods, but it can help distinguish between species that are otherwise alike in color, texture and weight. Although odor, like luster, is distinctive for only a few woods, it can be a useful key to identification, particularly among softwoods. Odor is most pronounced in freshly cut lumber,

and can be revived by moistening a dry wood sample.

Checking a sample for hardness by running a fingernail along the grain and noting the degree of indentation can help differentiate similar species such as butternut and black walnut.

The standard tool for macroscopic viewing of wood is a 10x hand lens. Choose one with built-in illumination for sharp resolution. Examine samples in good light, holding the lens close to one eye and moving the surface to be studied into focus. Note the distribution and shape of features such as vessels, tracheids, resin canals, earlywood, latewood, pores and medullary rays. The rela-

tive diameter of vessels (in hardwood) or tracheids (in softwood) is important in determining the texture of the wood; the larger these cells, the coarser the wood. The distribution of pores within the growth rings will also tell you whether a hardwood is ring-, diffuse-, semi-ring- or semi-diffuse-porous. When viewing end grain, choose an area of average growth rate, avoiding defects like cross grain and knots.

With softwoods, look for resin canals; they are only present in pine, spruce, larch and Douglas-fir. If you are looking for rays—an important feature of hardwoods—they are best seen on a transverse or tangential surface.

COMPARING MAGNIFIED VIEWS OF TWO WOOD SAMPLES

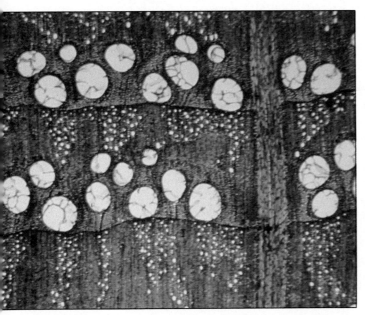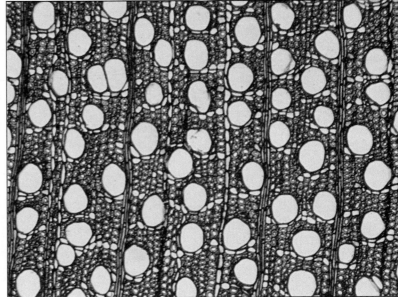

The two photos above show what the end grain, or transverse sections, of two different hardwood samples would look like under the magnification of a hand lens. A ring-porous hardwood (above, left) features rows of relatively large pores in the earlywood and clusters of smaller pores in the latewood. The vertical bars interrupting the pores are medullary rays. A semi-ring-porous wood (above, right) shows little distinction between the earlywood and latewood. Here, the pores are evenly distributed throughout the tissue.

WOOD IDENTIFICATION KEYS

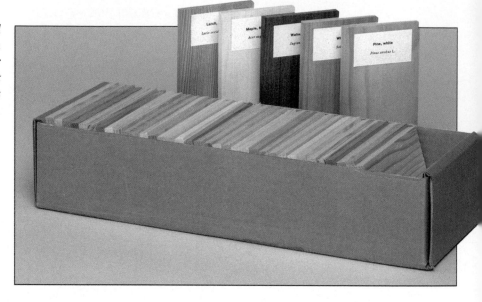

A collection of labeled wood samples can be invaluable in helping you become familiar with a variety of woods. It may also contain a species you wish to identify.

Correctly identifying an unfamiliar wood sample out of thousands of possibilities requires close observation, and a thorough knowledge of wood and its properties. But as a practical matter, the possible choices are usually limited to several familiar species, and a commercially available set of labeled wood samples, such as the one shown at right, may include a piece that matches the wood you are attempting to identify. Most often, however, you will need to record the features of a sample, then use a wood identification key from a book to make sense of your results.

An identification key is essentially a master list of woods and their properties that serves as a cross-reference to link the features of a particular sample to a species name. Some keys require that you compare their entries against features that are visible to the naked eye or with a 10x magnifier, while others demand that you note microscopic details. Still other keys are based on the user having wide-ranging sensory information about the wood, including its color, odor and texture, and the bark and leaf shape of the tree from which it came.

Using a key is like climbing the branches of a tree. You are asked to answer a series of paired statements, choosing the one that best describes the wood in question and proceeding to the next pair indicated. At each statement, the user forks onto a different branch until reaching a leaf that identifies the sample. The first statement may involve the texture of the wood. If the wood is porous, for example, you are sent to one set of statements; if it is non-porous, you jump to a different set of statements. You continue this way, flipping from page to page in a book, as each answer gradually reduces the choices. Finally, the search is narrowed to a single species.

Avoid keys that try to cover every wood species in the world; they will prove too general. Choose one that describes trees in a specific region, such as North American softwoods or tropical hardwoods. Several classic keys can be found in woodworking books; check your local library or bookstore. Some public agencies *(below)* also offer wood identification services.

SOURCES FOR WOOD IDENTIFICATION

Books

Edlin, Herbert L., *What Wood Is That? A Manual of Wood Identification.* New York: Viking, 1969.

Hoadley, Bruce, *Identifying Wood.* Newton, Connecticut: Taunton Press, 1990.

Panshin, A.J. and DeZeeuw, Carl, *Textbook of Wood Technology.* New York: McGraw Hill, 1980.

Rendle, B.J., *World Timbers: Volumes 1-3.* London: Ernest Benn, 1970.

Sharp, John B., *Wood Identification: A Manual for The Non-Professional.* Knoxville: University of Tennessee

Agricultural Extension Service, Forestry and Wildlife Extension, 1990.

Timber Research Development Association, *Timbers of the World: Volumes 1 and 2.* Lancaster: Construction Press, 1979.

Agencies that offer wood identification services

Center For Wood Anatomy Research U.S. Forest Products Laboratory 1 Gifford Pinchot Drive Madison, Wisconsin 53705-2398

International Wood Collectors Society 2913 Third Street Trenton, Michigan 48183

USING A WOOD IDENTIFICATION KEY

Here is an example of how a typical wood identification key works. In this case, we are starting with a plain-sawn board of an unknown wood. The first step is aimed at narrowing the investigation to either the hardwood or the softwood portion of the key. You examine your sample with a hand lens and observe that it has vessels and is porous; according to your key, it is a hardwood. Next, you must determine whether the wood is ring- or diffuse-porous: You notice that its earlywood is not sharply defined; you are told that it is diffuse-porous. The next features to examine are the rays. Seen in the tangential view of your sample, the rays are relatively narrow and uniform in width. This observation leads to another concerning the size of the pores in the growth rings. Since the pores in the earlywood of your sample are larger than those in the latewood, this indicates that you have a semi-diffuse-porous wood. Next, you examine the distribution of the pores in the growth ring. If they were unevenly distributed, the key would identify your sample as tanoak. Instead, the pores in your sample are evenly distributed. You must then evaluate the storage cells in the latewood. Seeing that they are present in a fine, unbroken line, you are directed to determine the color of the heartwood. If it were chestnut-brown or chocolate, you would have a piece of black walnut or butternut. But since the heartwood is brown to yellow-brown, you have either water hickory or persimmon. Since the rays of your sample are stacked vertically, creating ripple marks, the key leads you to the end of your quest: the sample is persimmon.

Wood without stacked rays; storage cells conspicuous in continuous lines throughout latewood: Water hickory

Wood with stacked rays, forming ripple marks extending across the grain when tangential section of wood is viewed: Persimmon

Heartwood chestnut-brown to chocolate or purplish brown

Heartwood brown to yellow-brown

Latewood storage cells appear in fine, continuous lines

Latewood storage cells not evident

Pores evenly distributed throughout growth ring

Pores unevenly distributed throughout growth ring and found in clusters separated by sections of fibrous tissue: Tanoak

Pores in the earlywood larger than those in the latewood; transition gradual (semi-diffuse-porous)

Pores uniform in size throughout the ring

Rays broad and visible

Rays narrow and uniform in width

Wood ring-porous (earlywood sharply defined); earlywood pores larger than latewood pores and visible to the naked eye

Wood diffuse-porous (earlywood not sharply defined); earlywood pores smaller than latewood pores and visible to the naked eye

Wood non-porous (without vessels): Wood tissue dominated by tracheids in distinct rows; rays not visible to the naked eye

Wood porous (with vessels): Wood tissue dominated by vessels (pores) embedded in fibrous tissue; rays may or may not be visible to the naked eye

START HERE

PORTABLE LUMBER MILLS

The desire to gain a deeper understanding of wood eventually leads some woodworkers out of the shop and lumberyard, into the woods, and back to the tree itself. By sawing your own lumber from logs, you can produce boards that exactly meet a project's specifications and gain valuable insight into wood as a living material. Each step yields a thrill of discovery as you watch patterns of grain and figure emerge from the log.

A number of lumber mills on the market allow you to cut through-and-through cut, plain-sawn or quartersawn boards. These tools include large stationary production mills capable of cutting logs more than 20 feet in length, portable models with tough band saw blades, and still smaller units that use chain saws.

The procedures that follow show you how to cut logs into lumber with a chain saw that is guided by a jig that attaches to it. Besides the cutting jig and a heavy-duty saw, this simple method requires nothing more than a straight board, a hammer and a few nails.

Most chain saws are designed to crosscut trees—that is, buck the logs into shorter lengths after the trees are felled and delimbed. Cutting logs into lumber is a ripping operation in which the sawing is done along the length of the log. Ripping with a chain saw requires at least three times as much power as crosscutting, and the saw must run at full throttle throughout most of the cut. Because much portable lumber milling involves hardwood logs, it is best to use a direct-drive chain saw rated at a speed of at least 3000 feet per minute, with a rip-ping chain installed. To minimize strain on the saw, try to select logs that are relatively free of defects such as twist and taper, with few knots and burls.

Felling trees and cutting logs with a chain saw is dangerous work requiring safe working habits. Pay attention to your task at all times and keep cutting edges sharp, clean and well maintained.

Since prolonged work with chain saws can damage the ears, wear hearing protection, such as earplugs or ear muffs. Proper dress for chain saw work also includes a full-face shield and steel-toed boots; do not wear loose clothing. You can also don special chain saw gloves to protect your hands and a pair of safety chaps made from a tough, synthetic fiber, such as Kevlar™, to protect your legs should the saw accidentally slip or jump back.

Specialized commercial jigs and machines enable you to cut logs into lumber. Here, a band saw lumber mill cuts a 2-by-10 board from a squared-off log. The device features a narrow-kerf blade that produces less waste than a chain saw, making it feasible to cut planks as narrow as ¼ inch thick without excessive waste.

CUTTING A LOG INTO BOARDS

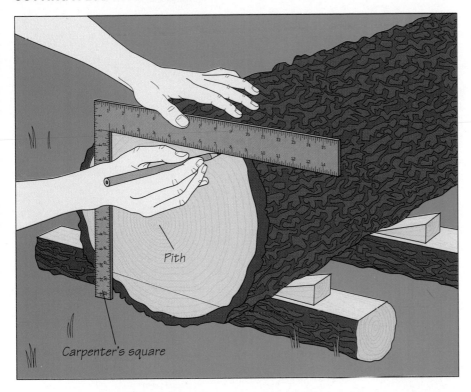

Carpenter's square

Pith

1 Squaring the log
To mark out the cant—the squared-off part of the log—and maximize the number of boards the log will yield, scribe a square on both ends of the log. Start at the end with the smallest diameter. Place the inside angle of a carpenter's square just inside the bark, and mark two outside edges of the square with a pencil. Using the scribed lines as a guide, complete the square *(left)*. Measure the sides of the square and transfer them to the other end of the log, making sure that the pith is centered in the square.

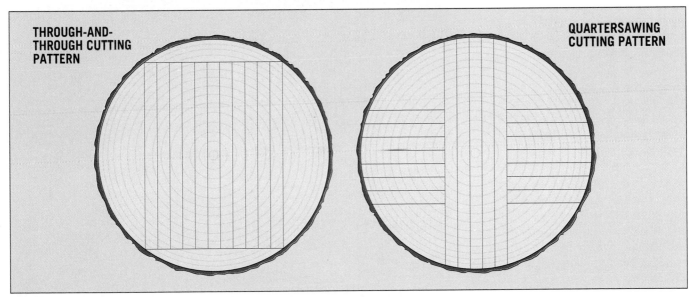

THROUGH-AND-THROUGH CUTTING PATTERN

QUARTERSAWING CUTTING PATTERN

2 Choosing the cutting pattern
Before cutting the log, choose between through-and-through cut and quartersawing and mark out the appropriate cutting pattern on the ends of the log. For through-and-through cut lumber *(above, left)*, scribe a series of lines within the square so that the board faces are roughly tangent to the growth rings. Space the lines according to the board thickness you want. For quartersawn lumber *(above, right)*, divide the square into three segments. Mark out the middle segment as for through-and-through cut lumber, then scribe lines in the two outside segments that are perpendicular to those in the middle. The growth rings will be more or less perpendicular to the faces of these boards.

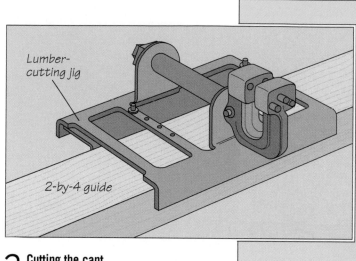

Lumber-cutting jig

2-by-4 guide

Spacer

3 Cutting the cant

Set the log on spacers, with one side of the marked square vertical. Cut a 2-by-4 guide longer than the log, then position it on top of the log so that it extends beyond each end. Align the outside edge of the guide with the side of the square and nail it in place. Use wood shims to level the guide. Place the lumber-cutting jig on the guide *(above)* and adjust its fence so that it runs smoothly along the guide. Attach the chain saw to the jig following the manufacturer's instructions. To make the cut, position the jig on the guide at the smallest end of the log. Then, with the saw blade clear of the log, start up the saw and tip it forward so that the blade bites into the log. Carefully step backwards and draw the jig along the guide, cutting through the log to the other end. To cut the other sides, remove the guide and rotate the log. Repeat the procedure to align the guide with the square and make the cut *(right)*. Continue until all the sides are cut. To cut the resulting cant into boards, use the chain saw and the jig to cut along the lines you marked in step 2. If you have a band saw, you can cut the log into a manageable 6-by-6 cant with the chain saw, then use the band saw to cut the cant into boards. With its narrower kerf, a band saw blade produces less waste than a chain saw blade.

BUILD IT YOURSELF

LOG CROSSCUTTING JIG

Simplify the task of squaring the ends of a log before cutting it into lumber with the crosscutting jig shown at right. The jig, which can be built to fit a variety of log sizes, consists of a guide and an inverted L-shaped frame with two triangular support brackets.

To make the jig, cut two pieces of ¾-inch plywood for the frame. The lengths of the pieces should exceed the diameter of the largest log you expect to handle. The width of the top piece should equal the desired width of cut. Screw the two pieces together along with the triangular brackets. Screw a 2-by-4 guide that is at least 8 inches longer than the diameter of the log to the top piece, aligning its edge with that of the top piece.

To use the jig, set the log on spacers and position the jig atop the log. Nail the side piece of the frame to the end of the log, making sure that the guide is level and square to the log's axis. Set up the chain saw and the lumber-cutting jig on the guide as you would to cut a log into a cant *(page 38)*. Then start the saw and tip it forward so that the blade bites into the log *(right, below)*. Draw the jig along the guide until you cut through the log. At the end of the cut, the crosscutting jig and the cutoff piece will topple toward you. Keep the blade from binding in the kerf and stand clear of the jig at the end of the cut.

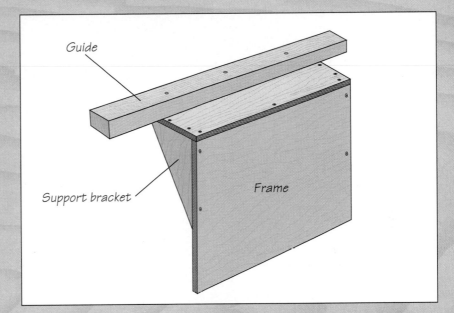

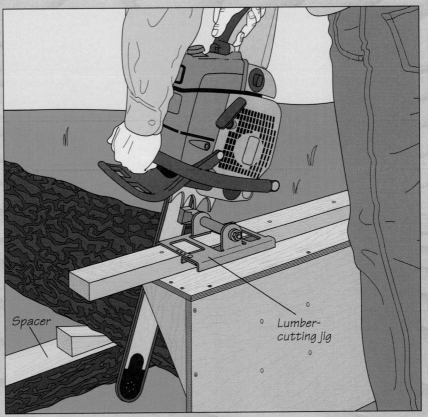

SELECTING LUMBER

Principal tool of the lumber grader's trade, a lumber ruler measures the width of a board. With a flexible shaft and a hook at one end for flipping stock, the ruler enables a grader to fill an order for wood quickly.

Some craftsmen buy their wood project by project. They design and lay out a piece of furniture, calculate the amount and type of wood required, then embark on a quest for exactly what they need. Other woodworkers stockpile beautiful or interesting pieces of wood even before they have a specific project in mind. Picking through the piles at the local wood dealership, surveying felled logs at a building site or scavenging bucked logs left over from roadside tree work, these craftsmen accumulate promising wood in the drying shed—a supply that serves as an inspiration for future work.

Whatever your approach, there are several sources to cover in your search for raw materials. The most obvious is the local lumberyard. Some yards stock specialty items, depending on demand in the areas they service; lumberyards along the coast, for example, might carry mahogany and teak for boat construction and repair. But because most yards primarily supply the construction trades, your solid-wood choices will probably be limited to structural softwood lumber and perhaps an occasional piece of oak. For a wider choice of hardwoods, and for wood carving and turning blanks, you will have to range farther afield. Look in the Yellow Pages for dealerships that specialize in fine hardwoods, or scan the advertisements in woodworking magazines for mail-order woodworking-supply companies.

You will pay top dollar for hardwoods bought from a retail source, but in return you will generally receive material that has been graded for quality using the standards established by the National Hardwood Lumber Association. In addition, some care has probably been taken to control the moisture content of the stock during its stay in the yard. You can also ask the retailer to furnish stock that is surfaced to a uniform thickness—a necessity for woodworkers who do not have access to a power planer.

There are other, less costly ways to obtain wood. If you live near a small sawmill, you may find good quality lumber at a very low price. However, the wood will probably be green, rough and ungraded—and it must be stickered, seasoned and surfaced before it can be used for furniture. Bigger sawmills prefer to deal with large volumes of wood and may be reluctant to fill small orders. One answer is to pool your material needs with those of other woodworkers. Some sawmills will sell you their "planer outs"—small pieces of varying widths and thicknesses that can be bought at bargain prices.

It may also be economical for you to buy wood that has been recycled after many years of use in barns, factories, wharves and other structures. You may also find an opportunity to do your own recycling. Reusing old wood makes sense environmentally, and it is rapidly becoming the only legal way of obtaining some species. In addition, recycled boards that were cut from straight-grained old-growth timber may be superior to fresh lumber cut from smaller trees. There are drawbacks to recycling wood, however. Wear, rot and insects may add up to a waste factor of 50 percent or more. And you should expect to extract many nails, bolts and staples—and still ruin saw blades in encounters with hidden metal.

Different grades of lumber can vary widely—even in the same stack of boards. There is no more certain way of getting what you want than selecting the stock yourself.

ORDERING LUMBER

When it is time to order lumber for a project, it pays to do your homework before you go to the lumberyard. By becoming an informed and well-organized consumer, you increase your odds of coming away with your needs met and your wallet intact. You will also avoid having to make extra trips to your supplier.

• **Species:** Ask for a specific wood species, not merely a broad family name. For example, order "white oak," not just "oak." Every species has unique properties; select one with the characteristics that suit the needs of your project. It can be helpful to learn the basics of wood identification *(page 30)*, since at some lumberyards several similar types of woods may be lumped together under the same name.

• **Quantity:** Lumber may be ordered either by the linear foot or the board foot. Be sure your supplier knows which measure you are using, because they are very different. Board-foot calculations, which actually describe a volume of wood, are explained at the bottom of the next page. As a general rule, you can order stock of like dimension by the linear foot—25 linear feet of 1-by-4 lumber, for example. The main limitation of this method, however, is that it only works with lumber of uniform width and thickness. Once you mix dimensions—as you probably will end up doing when ordering hardwood—a board foot measurement becomes necessary to describe your needs.

How you order your wood can also depend on whether you need softwood or hardwood. With softwoods you can usually specify any board width or length, while hardwood boards are generally available in random widths and lengths, depending on the grade you order.

• **Size:** Wood is sold in nominal rather than real sizes, so remember to make allowances for the difference when ordering surfaced lumber. A 1-by-6 piece of pine, for example, is actually ¾ inch thick and 5½ inches wide when dried and surfaced. With rough, or unsurfaced green lumber, the nominal and real sizes are the same. For more information on how nominal and real sizes compare, refer to the charts on pages 46 (hardwoods) and 48 (softwoods).

The thickness of hardwood boards is commonly expressed as a non-reduced fraction in quarters of an inch. A 1-inch-thick oak board, for example, is termed ⁴⁄₄ lumber, a 1½-inch-thick plank is ⁶⁄₄ and so on.

• **Grade:** When ordering a particular grade of wood, use standard terminology. Refer to the chart on page 47 for hardwoods and on page 49 for softwoods. The main differences between higher and lower hardwood grades lie in appearance rather than strength. In general, reserve higher-grade wood for the visible parts of your projects.

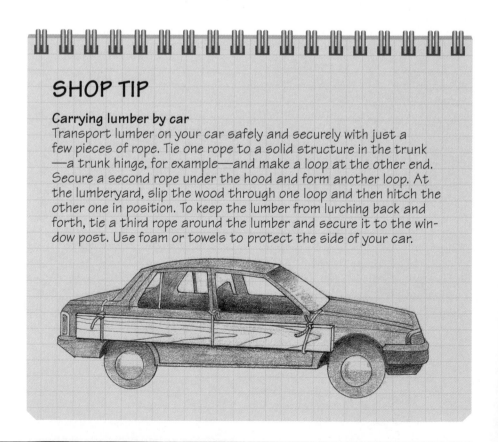

SHOP TIP

Carrying lumber by car
Transport lumber on your car safely and securely with just a few pieces of rope. Tie one rope to a solid structure in the trunk —a trunk hinge, for example—and make a loop at the other end. Secure a second rope under the hood and form another loop. At the lumberyard, slip the wood through one loop and then hitch the other one in position. To keep the lumber from lurching back and forth, tie a third rope around the lumber and secure it to the window post. Use foam or towels to protect the side of your car.

• **Seasoning:** Lumber is sold either kiln-dried (KD) or air-dried (AD). The practical difference between the two is that KD wood has a lower moisture content—about 8 percent, while air-dried, high-density hardwoods generally have a moisture content range of 20 to 25 percent. Softwoods and lower-density hardwoods are air-dried to 15 to 20 percent moisture content. KD lumber is therefore preferable for making indoor furniture, because the wood is unlikely to dry out any further; as well, the kiln's heat allows the wood's cells to reposition, reducing the likelihood of warping and checking. This does not mean you need to restrict yourself to buying only KD lumber, however; in fact, many carvers prefer moister wood, making AD wood a better choice for them. You can bring air-dried wood to the appropriate moisture level for cabinetmaking, as shown in the Drying and Storing Wood chapter *(page 78)*.

• **Surfacing:** Also known as dressing, surfacing refers to how lumber has been prepared at the mill before it is sent to the lumberyard. Lumber that is surfaced is usually surfaced on both sides: S2S lumber has been planed smooth on both faces, while S4S wood has had both faces planed and both edges jointed. Rough, or unsurfaced, lumber (Rgh) is less expensive than either S2S or S4S wood, and if you own a planer and a jointer, you can save money by surfacing rough lumber in your shop *(page 53)*.

A sample order for wood at a lumberyard might be as follows: 100 bd. ft. ⁸/₄ FAS red oak, S2S. This would amount to 100 board feet of nominally 2-inch-thick FAS (Firsts and Seconds) grade red oak with both faces planed smooth.

Once you receive your lumber, check it carefully to make sure you are getting what you want. If the order does not meet your specifications, do not feel obliged to buy it.

CALCULATING BOARD FEET

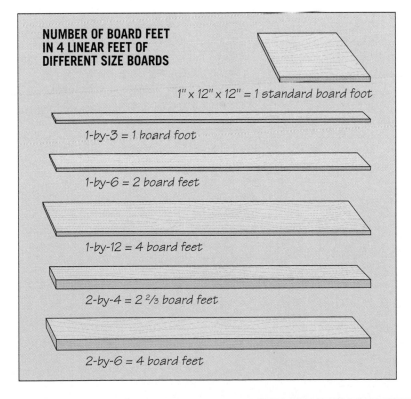

NUMBER OF BOARD FEET IN 4 LINEAR FEET OF DIFFERENT SIZE BOARDS

1" x 12" x 12" = 1 standard board foot

1-by-3 = 1 board foot

1-by-6 = 2 board feet

1-by-12 = 4 board feet

2-by-4 = 2 ²/₃ board feet

2-by-6 = 4 board feet

Ordering lumber by the board foot

Because the board foot is a unit of measurement that offers a standard way of totaling the volume of stock regardless of dimensions, it is commonly used when dealing with lumber. As shown at left, the standard board foot is equivalent to a piece that is 1 inch thick, 12 inches wide and 12 inches long. To calculate the number of board feet in a particular piece of wood, multiply its three dimensions together. Then divide the result by 144 if the dimensions are all in inches, or by 12 if one dimension is expressed in feet. For the standard board, the formula is:
1" x 12" x 12" ÷ 144 = 1 (or 1" x 12" x 1' ÷ 12 = 1).
So if you had an 8-foot-long 1-by-3, you would calculate the board feet as follows: 1 x 3 x 8 ÷ 12 = 2 (or 2 board feet). Other examples are shown in the illustration. Remember that board feet are calculated on the basis of nominal rather than actual sizes.

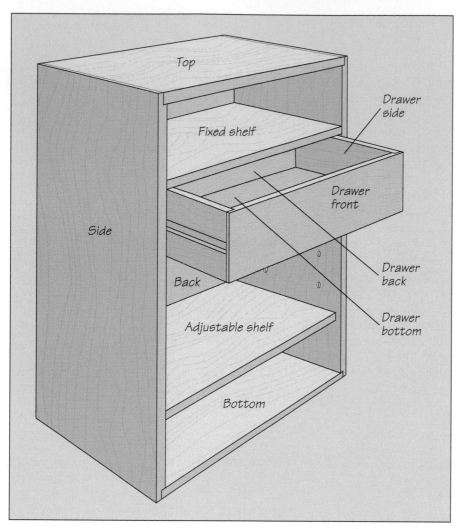

Top

Drawer side

Fixed shelf

Drawer front

Side

Back

Drawer back

Adjustable shelf

Drawer bottom

Bottom

Making and using a cutting list

A cutting list records the finished sizes of the lumber needed for a particular project. It may be included with the plans you purchase; otherwise, you will have to fashion your own based on a drawing of the design. Tally up the number of board feet for each piece using the formula shown on page 43; tack on an extra 30 to 40 percent to account for defects in the wood and waste. For the project shown on this page, which totals roughly 16 board feet, you should order at least 20 or 25 board feet of ⁴/₄ lumber in addition to the necessary quantity of plywood sheeting. The cutting list should include the name of the part, the quantity, the dimensions of the pieces and the kind of wood suitable for the project. For convenience, assign a letter to each piece.

CUTTING LIST						
Piece	Qty.	L.	W.	Th.	Material	Board feet
A Top	1	23¼	13	1	ash	2.10
B Bottom	1	23¼	13	1	ash	2.10
C Side	2	32	13	1	ash	5.78
D Fixed shelf	1	23¼	13	1	ash	2.10
E Adjustable shelf	1	22⅜	12½	1	ash	1.94
F Drawer front	1	22¼	5	1	ash	.77
G Drawer side	2	11½	5	1	ash	.80
H Drawer back	1	21¼	5	1	ash	.74
I Drawer bottom	1	21¼	10	¼	plywood	—
J Back	1	32	24	¼	plywood	—

GRADING LUMBER

Lumber grading is a way of evaluating the surface quality of a board according to certain standards, taking into account factors such as the number, size and degree of defects in the wood. The goal is to ensure that woodworkers get what they pay for; a board of a certain grade of wood bought in Maine will closely resemble a similar-grade board purchased in New Mexico.

At first glance, the rules of grading may seem arbitrary. For starters, the standards are different for softwoods and hardwoods, the result of the end use of each type of wood. Softwoods are primarily used in construction, so a grader may assume that a softwood board will be used as is, with no further surfacing. Hardwood boards, on the other hand, are almost always planed, crosscut and ripped into smaller pieces to fit

a particular piece of furniture. Added to that is the fact that, while there is one standard for hardwoods, softwoods are further divided into separate groups and graded according to rules established by different organizations.

Taking the time to become familiar with hardwood and softwood grading will pay dividends. A sound understanding of the grading system enables you to select the most appropriate board for the job at hand; it can also save you money. There is no need, for example, to order long planks of top-grade FAS (or Firsts and Seconds) lumber if most of the pieces of the cabinet you intend to build are only three or four feet long. You would probably be better off buying No. 1 Common, which is considerably cheaper, and will be adequate once you have cut out the defects.

Lumber producers and vendors have long found it advantageous to study wood types and set rules for grading to guarantee a uniform product. One of the earliest instances of grading occurred in 1764, when Sven Aversdon of Stockholm divided Swedish pine into four categories—best, good, common and culls. During the 18th Century, appearance was the primary criterion for grading wood, but as knowledge of wood properties increased, standards changed to include strength and the amount of clear or usable wood in each board.

The best way to become familiar with grades is to visit a lumberyard and examine stock firsthand. Get to know how a hardwood grade like FAS differs from No. 1 Common. And when you Select lumber, try to picture how each part can be cut out of a board with the least waste.

HARDWOOD LUMBER GRADER'S EVALUATION OF A TYPICAL BOARD

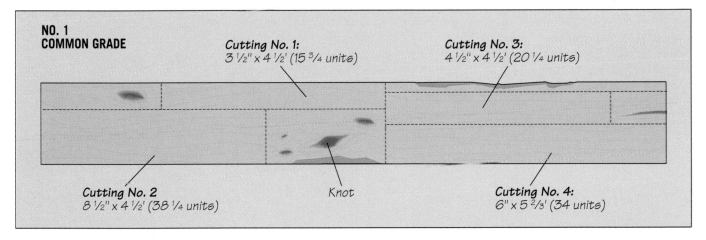

NO. 1 COMMON GRADE

Cutting No. 1:
3 1/2" x 4 1/2' (15 3/4 units)

Cutting No. 3:
4 1/2" x 4 1/2' (20 1/4 units)

Cutting No. 2
8 1/2" x 4 1/2' (38 1/4 units)

Knot

Cutting No. 4:
6" x 5 2/3' (34 units)

Equipped with lumber rule, pen and log book, a professional lumber grader can evaluate a hardwood board in roughly 15 seconds. Although the system is scientific, it is not foolproof. Grading is all done by eye—the eye of a human grader. Still, rigid quality control ensures that only a very small percentage of boards are not graded correctly.

Here are the four basic steps lumber graders take to make their assessment:

1. Determine the species and multiply the length by the width of the board to find the surface measure (SM) in square feet—in the board above, 12 inches (1 foot) x 12 feet = 12 SM.

2. Choose the poorest face from which to grade and visualize

the number of imaginary defect-free cuts that can be made; in this case, 4.

3. Determine the number of portions of cutting units—clear lumber 1" wide by 1' long—that can be made from the 4 cuts; in this case, 108 1/4. (If the board were perfect, it would yield 144 cutting units.)

4. Consult a chart that lists the qualities of different grades and factor in the number of cutting units and the number of allowable cuts: A No. 1 Common board requires that two thirds of the total cutting units are clear. Given the size of this particular board, up to 4 cuts would be allowed. Since this board meets both criteria, it justifies the grade No. 1 Common.

HARDWOOD GRADES

A hundred years ago, hardwood grading varied from mill to mill, but with the formation of the National Hardwood Lumber Association (NHLA) in 1898, grading became standardized. At first, the rules were based strictly on the number and size of defects; in 1932 they were broadened to reflect the proportion of a board that can be cut into smaller pieces, called cuttings. These pieces must be clear on one side and sound on the other. Their size also determines the grade. Today's hardwood grading standards assume that boards are invariably cut into smaller pieces to make furniture; thus, grade is based on a board's poorest face, except in the case of Select, which takes the board's best face into account.

Select is one of seven standard hardwood grades. The top grade is FAS (an abbreviation of Firsts and Seconds), followed by Select, No. 1 Common, No. 2A and 2B Common, and No. 3A Common and No. 3B Common (*chart, opposite*). No. 2A and No. 2B Common are frequently lumped together as No. 2 Common; likewise, many lumberyards sell No. 3A and No. 3B Common together as No. 3 Common.

The better the grade, the higher the percentage of clear cuttings: 83⅓ percent of Select boards must be clear face cuttings; only 50 percent of a No. 2 Common board need be defect-free. But grading is a more subtle art than these calculations indicate. Two boards that are the same size with the same number of defects can end up in different grades: The position of the defects may prevent one board from having large enough clear cuttings to make the higher grade of the other board.

Although paying more for better-grade stock means that you will end up with wood having fewer defects, this may not always be the economical thing to do. If your project is relatively modest, hand-pick the lumber yourself from a variety of grades, depending on the function of each board in the piece. Where only one defect-free face is called for, the select grade is a good choice. Or, for the pieces of your furniture project that are relatively small, for example, you may be able to get by with No. 1 Common grade boards. No. 2A Common boards are suitable for the parts of projects in which appearance is not of paramount importance, such as hidden furniture frames. If you do buy lower-grade lumber, however, plan on more waste when you are calculating the number of board feet to order.

Of course, beauty is in the eye of the beholder. Some cabinetmakers feel that defects such as knots add character to a piece of furniture. And if most of the parts will end up being small, lower-grade wood is not only more economical, it may also be more suitable for the task at hand—by yielding more attractively figured wood.

STANDARD THICKNESS FOR SURFACED HARDWOOD	
Nominal (rough)	**Actual (surfaced two sides)**
3/8"	3/16"
1/2"	5/16"
5/8"	7/16"
3/4"	9/16"
1"	3/4" or 13/16"
1¼"	1 1/16"
1½"	1 5/16"
2"	1½" or 1¾"
3"	2¾"
4"	3¾"

These two oak boards demonstrate the range of hardwood grades. The top board contains knots and is classified as No. 2A Common; the bottom board is defect-free FAS grade lumber.

HARDWOOD LUMBER GRADES

GRADE	FAS	SELECT	NO. 1 COMMON	NO. 2A & 2B COMMON	NO. 3A COMMON	NO. 3B COMMON
Allowable length of board	8' - 16'	6' - 16'	4' - 16'	4' - 16'	4' - 16'	4' - 16'
Allowable width of board	6" or wider	4" or wider	3" or wider	3" or wider	3" or wider	3" or wider
Minimum % of clear face cuttings	83⅓%	83⅓%	66⅔%	50%	33⅓%	25%
Minimum size of clear cuttings	3" x 7'; 4" x 5'	3" x 7'; 4" x 5'	3" x 3'; 4" x 2'	3" x 2'	3" x 2'	Not less than 1½" wide containing 36 square inches
Formula to determine number of cuts	SM ÷ 4	SM ÷ 4	SM+1 ÷ 3	SM ÷ 2	–	–
Maximum number of clear cuttings permitted	4	4	5	7	Unlimited	Unlimited

Reading the chart

This chart, created by the National Hardwood Lumber Association (NHLA), records the minimum requirements a board must meet to merit a particular grade. Generally, a higher-grade board is longer, wider and more defect-free than one of a lesser grade. The clear pieces are obtained with as few cuts as possible.

By comparing the dimensions of a board with the figures supplied in the chart, it is possible to determine the grade of a particular piece of lumber. The first two horizontal rows provide data on minimum board dimensions for each grade. The third row gives information on the percentage of defect-free surface, or clear face cuttings, a board must have for each grade. The minimum size of each clear face cutting is listed in row four. Once the surface area, or surface measure (SM), of a board is determined, the formula in row 5 will give the total number of cuttings allowed for a particular grade. Row 6 contains the number of clear cuttings each grade permits.

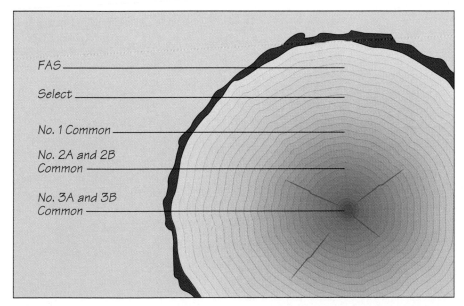

FAS
Select
No. 1 Common
No. 2A and 2B Common
No. 3A and 3B Common

The location of lumber grades on a log

High grades of lumber, such as FAS and Select, are generally cut from the outer part of the log, near the bark. No. 3 Common grades, found closer to the pith, are not always suitable for cabinetmaking and are frequently used for packing crates or pallets. In some species, such as walnut, where color is important, the sapwood does not qualify as top grade, even though it may be clear.

SOFTWOOD GRADES

Although cabinetmakers generally prefer hardwoods, many fine pieces of furniture have been built with softwood. There are good reasons for using hardwood's less expensive cousin: Softwood is generally more readily available than hardwood, and is easy to work.

Pine is one of the most popular choices of cabinetmakers. Its varieties include Eastern white pine, Southern yellow pine and species from the West, such as sugar pine, Idaho white pine and ponderosa pine. Douglas-fir, another Western softwood, is also gaining popularity as a cabinet wood. Sitka spruce and Western larch are two other good choices.

For cabinetmaking, you should restrict yourself to grades of softwood shown in the chart on the following page. Remember that softwoods are generally sold S4S—that is, planed smooth on both faces and jointed on the edges. And they are graded based on the board's best face after surfacing.

Unlike hardwoods, softwoods are graded differently depending on the species; the grade for a California redwood board, for example, does not apply to a piece of ponderosa pine. You can obtain information about softwood grading standards from the American Lumber Standards Committee in Germantown, Maryland.

Softwood grading takes both strength and appearance into account. Three grade categories—Select, Finish and Common—are often used for woodworking. Select and Finish grades must

This French-Canadian nightstand was built entirely with pine—an attractive alternative to more expensive hardwoods.

be clear of defects, while boards in the Common grades may contain defects such as tight knots. Select and Finish stock are seasoned to a moisture content of 15 percent or less. Common boards, used mainly in construction and home-building, may have up to a 19 percent moisture level. The quality of Common grade boards is further divided into categories 1 to 5, with the highest number corresponding to the lowest grade.

Some boards display a grade stamp, like the one shown on page 49. The stamp displays information about the species, moisture content when surfaced and grade of the stock. To avoid marring their appearance, however, 1-inch-thick boards in the better grades are often not stamped after surfacing. The stamp may also be missing from lesser grade boards that have been cut into shorter lengths by retail lumber dealers.

Keep in mind that softwood is sold according to nominal size, or green dimensions, which is different from a board's actual size. A 2-by-4, for example, actually measures 1½ by 3½ inches. The chart below shows nominal sizes of some commonly available boards along with their true sizes when surfaced.

NOMINAL AND ACTUAL SOFTWOOD LUMBER SIZES

NOMINAL (INCHES)	ACTUAL (INCHES)	
	Surfaced dry	Surfaced green
1-by-2	¾-by-1½	²⁵/₃₂-by-1⁹/₁₆
1-by-3	¾-by-2½	²⁵/₃₂-by-2⁹/₁₆
1-by-4	¾-by-3½	²⁵/₃₂-by-3⁹/₁₆
1-by-6	¾-by-5½	²⁵/₃₂-by-5⅝
1-by-8	¾-by-7¼	²⁵/₃₂-by-7½
1-by-10	¾-by-9¼	²⁵/₃₂-by-9½
1-by-12	¾-by-11¼	²⁵/₃₂-by-11½
2-by-2	1½-by-1½	1⁹/₁₆-by-1⁹/₁₆

NOMINAL (INCHES)	ACTUAL (INCHES)	
	Surfaced dry	Surfaced green
2-by-4	1½-by-3½	1⁹/₁₆-by-3⁹/₁₆
2-by-6	1½-by-5½	1⁹/₁₆-by-5⅝
2-by-8	1½-by-7¼	1⁹/₁₆-by-7½
2-by-10	1½-by-9¼	1⁹/₁₆-by-9½
2-by-12	1½-by-11¼	1⁹/₁₆-by-11½
3-by-4	2½-by-3½	2⁹/₁₆-by-3⁹/₁₆
4-by-4	3½-by-3½	3⁹/₁₆-by-3⁹/₁₆
4-by-6	3½-by-5½	3⁹/₁₆-by-5⅝

SOFTWOOD LUMBER GRADES FOR CABINETMAKING

GRADES	CHARACTERISTICS
Select B and BTR (supreme)	Clear appearance and highest quality; minor defects and blemishes. Ideal with clear finishes. Not always available; expensive
C Select (choice)	High quality; small defects and blemishes
D Select (quality)	Good quality; defects and blemishes more pronounced
Superior Finish	Highest quality of finish grade lumber; minor defects and blemishes
Prime Finish	High quality with few defects and blemishes
No. 1 Common (colonial)	Has limited availability and size ranges; may have small tight knots, making this grade appropriate if a knotty appearance is desired
No. 2 Common (sterling)	Larger, coarser defects and blemishes; often used where a knotty appearance with strong character is desired

DECIPHERING A GRADE STAMP

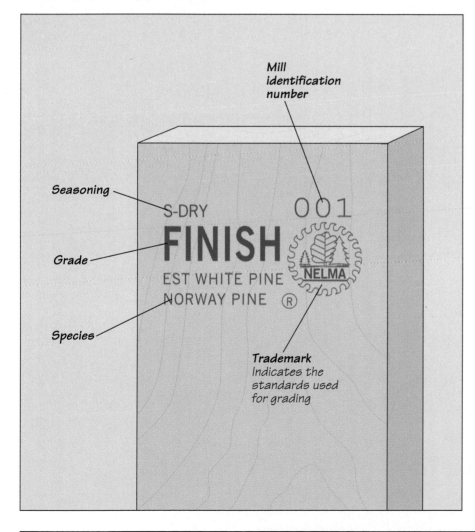

Mill identification number

Seasoning

Grade

Species

S-DRY

FINISH

EST WHITE PINE

NORWAY PINE ®

001

NELMA

Trademark
Indicates the standards used for grading

Reading a grade stamp
Most softwood grade stamps, like the one shown at left, contain five basic elements. A code number identifies the mill that produced the board, and the grade of the wood appears next to the trademark of the agency that established the rules for grading the wood (in this case, the Northeastern Lumber Manufacturers Association). The species is also noted; sometimes more than one species is stamped on the board, indicating it may be any of those listed. Finally, the seasoning information reflects the moisture content of the wood at the time it was surfaced: S-DRY means that the board was surfaced after seasoning and has no more than 19 percent moisture content; MC 15 refers to a board with a maximum moisture content of 15 percent; S-GRN is reserved for unseasoned wood surfaced with a moisture content above 19 percent. A board that has been surfaced while still green tends to shrink and its dimensions will not be as accurate as those of a board that has been surfaced after it was seasoned.

LUMBER DEFECTS

Most lumber defects adversely affect a board's appearance, strength, workability or ability to take a finish. Sometimes, however, irregularities or abnormalities can actually make a piece of wood more desirable, especially when they produce a popular, distinctive figure like bird's-eye or burl. Of course, intended use is the final arbiter; what may be a blemish to one woodworker is another board's selling point. Knots, for example, would be a significant defect in boards intended for a tabletop, but they are an essential feature of some types of paneling.

Lumber defects are either natural, man-made or the result of poor seasoning. All wood harbors natural defects that are caused by growing conditions or qualities of the species itself. The same type of defect may be present in different woods. Some imperfections are found in all species. Loose knots, for example, are caused simply by the way trees grow. They are the remnants of broken branches that have become encased by the growth of new wood. Other natural defects include gum in hardwoods, pitch in softwoods and reaction wood in all species. Natural forces such as fire, wind, fungi and insects can also cause defects in wood. A common defect of this sort is blue stain.

Several defects occur when wood is exposed to the air and allowed to dry. Because wood does not shrink uniformly in all dimensions, warping can result when the moisture content of lumber drops below a certain level. (Refer to the Drying and Storing Wood chapter for more information on proper seasoning of wood.) Some common seasoning defects are checks, bow, cup, twist, crook and split. Keep in mind that these defects can also occur in boards cut close to the pith of a log. Some common defects are explained in the chart below and opposite.

Although it is virtually impossible to buy wood that is completely defect-free, you can increase your chances of obtaining the best lumber for your needs by selecting your wood carefully *(page 42)*. Another point to consider is that you can salvage some lumber with defects if you have access to the necessary tools and learn how to use them *(page 53)*.

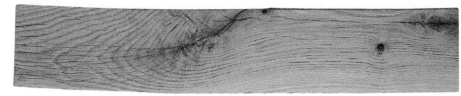

Three pieces of oak with defects: The top board shows splits, the middle piece reveals checks at one end, and the bottom board displays a crook, a loose knot and reaction wood.

DEFECTS IN WOOD

TYPE	CHARACTERISTICS	REMEDIES
Tight knot	Appears as a whorl that is intergrown with the surrounding wood tissue. Knots form as the girth of the tree increases, gradually enveloping the branches. If the branches are still alive at the time of their envelopment, the knot integrates with the wood in the tree trunk	Does not seriously weaken a board; can be cut out or used, as appearance dictates.
Loose or dead knot	Appears as a whorl encircled by a dark ring. When a branch dies the remaining stump is eventually enveloped by the trunk. But the dead stump cannot integrate with the tissue surrounding it, creating a loose or dead knot.	Remove knots before working with the lumber.

TYPE	CHARACTERISTICS	REMEDIES
Gum	An accumulation on the surface of the board or in pockets within the board. Usually develops when a tree has suffered an injury, exposure to fire or insect attack.	Do not use where a quality finish is required, as gum will bleed through most finishes.
Checks	Lengthwise ruptures or separations in the wood, usually caused by rapid drying. May compromise strength and appearance of board.	Can be cut off.
Bow	An end-to-end curve along the face, usually caused by improper storage of lumber. Introduces internal stresses in the wood that make it difficult to cut.	Flatten bowed boards on the jointer (page 55), or cut into shorter pieces, then use the jointer.
Cup	An edge-to-edge curve across the face, usually caused when one face of a board dries more quickly than the other. Common on tangentially cut stock, on boards cut close to the pith, or if one face of a board has less contact with the air than the other.	Cup may correct itself if both faces are allowed to dry to the same moisture content. Cupped boards can be salvaged on the band saw (page 54) or jointer (page 55).
Twist	Uneven or irregular warping where one corner is not aligned with the others. Results from uneven drying or a cross grain pattern that is not parallel to the edge.	Board can be salvaged on jointer (page 55), or cut into shorter boards.
Crook	End-to-end curve along the edge, caused by incorrect seasoning or having the pith of a log close to the board edge. Weakens the wood, making it unsuitable for weight-bearing applications.	Board can be salvaged on jointer or table saw (page 55).
Split	Similar to checks, appearing as separations along the growth rings. Also known as ring check or ring shank. Results from improper drying of wood or felling damage.	Board can be used, but split may mar the appearance of the wood, becoming more noticeable when stain is applied.
Machine burn	Appears as a dark streak across the faces or edges of lumber. Occurs when planer knives are dull or spin on one part of board for too long.	Remove machine burn with jointer (page 53) or sander.
Blue stain	Appears as a discoloration of the surface on otherwise normal-looking wood. Results from molds that flourish when lumber is dried or stored in warm, moist or poorly ventilated conditions. Species like holly and English sycamore are prone to blue stain.	Conceal with a dark stain.

THE STRESS OF UNEVEN GROWTH

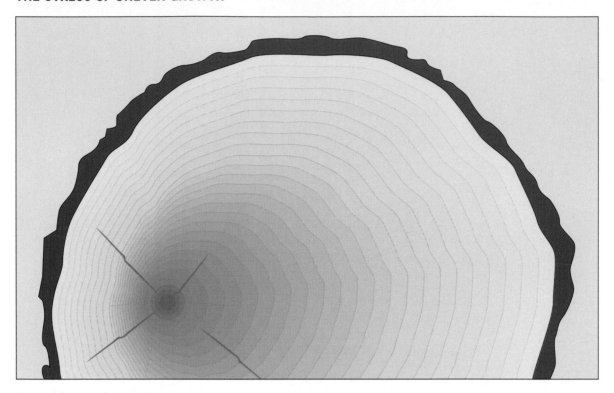

Recognizing reaction wood

Reaction wood, shown above, is characterized by its compressed growth rings and silvery, lifeless color. It occurs when a tree trunk has a pronounced curve, as often happens when a tree grows on a slope. This defect can also be seen in boards cut close to the pith of a trunk. Working with reaction wood poses problems for the woodworker; because it has different shrinkage properties than normal wood, the internal stresses in the board can cause a saw blade to bind and kick back. When the wood is cut or sanded, it has a fuzzy surface and absorbs stain unevenly. Bending reaction wood or placing any load on it may cause it to break across the grain.

SHOP TIP

Checking lumber for twist

Warped boards can sometimes be tough to recognize, but you can spot twisted stock quickly with the aid of shop-made winding sticks. Cut two narrow boards to a length that is twice the width of the board to be tested. Set the board face down on a work table, then place the winding sticks at both ends, parallel to each other. Sight across the tops of the sticks. Your board is twisted if the tops of the sticks are not perfectly aligned.

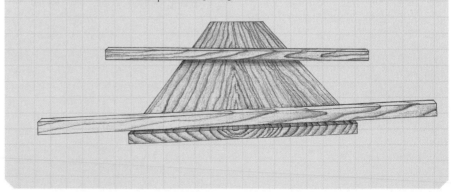

PREPARING LUMBER

The first job in a cabinetmaking project involves preparing your stock. If you own a jointer, a planer and a table saw, you can do the work yourself.

Whether to construct a large cabinet or a miniature jewelry box, lumber is generally prepared in the same way. The procedures you follow depend on how the wood was surfaced before you bought it. For rough boards, you start by smoothing one face on the jointer, then one edge. This will give you adjoining surfaces that are perfectly square to each other. Next, pass the second face through a planer so that the faces are parallel. Now you can rip your boards to width and crosscut them to length.

For S2S lumber, which has already had both faces surfaced, you need only pass one edge across the jointer, then rip and crosscut. S4S wood, with all four surfaces dressed, can be cut to width and length immediately; only edges that will be glued together need to be jointed.

Although lumber with defects should be avoided, you may find yourself with a few warped boards you do not want to discard. Several simple techniques for salvaging defective stock are shown on pages 54 and 55. A cupped board can be ripped into several narrower pieces, in effect flattening the curve into strips that can be jointed. A crooked or bowed board can be salvaged on the jointer by gradually cutting away the high spots. And a simple jig can be used with the table saw to transform a board with an uneven edge into a square piece.

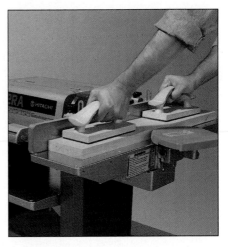

For surfacing a board face, push blocks help to keep stock flat and your hands safe. Lateral pressure keeps the edge against the fence.

SURFACING STOCK

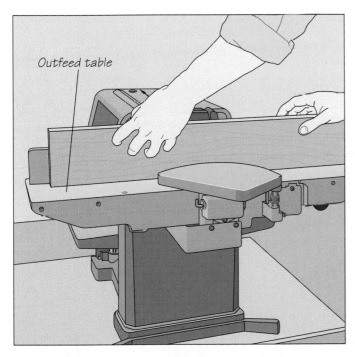

Outfeed table

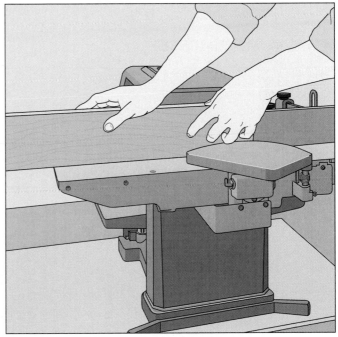

Jointing a board
Set a cutting depth between 1/16 and 1/8 inch. Joint a board face as shown in the photo above. To joint an edge, feed the stock slowly across the cutterhead, making sure that the knives are cutting with the grain *(page 29)*. While feeding the workpiece over the knives, use a hand-over-hand motion to keep downward pressure on the piece just to the outfeed side of the cutterhead, maintaining pressure against the fence. Continue these movements until you finish the cut.

Planing stock

Set a cutting depth up to $\frac{1}{16}$ inch. Stand to one side of the planer and use both hands to feed the stock carefully into the machine, keeping the board edges parallel to the edges of the planer table. Once the machine grips the board and begins pulling it across the cutterhead, support the trailing end to keep it flat on the table *(right)*. As the cut progresses, move to the outfeed side of the planer and support the piece with both hands until it clears the outfeed roller. If you are making several passes to reduce the board's thickness, plane the same amount of wood from both faces. This will minimize warping.

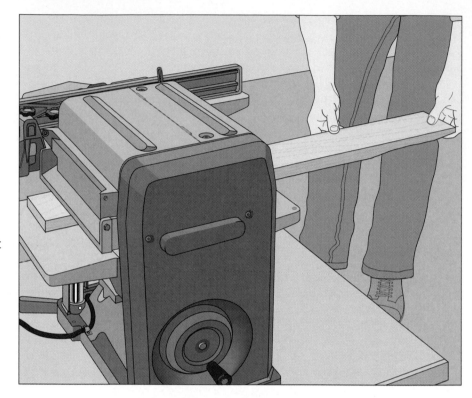

SALVAGING WARPED LUMBER

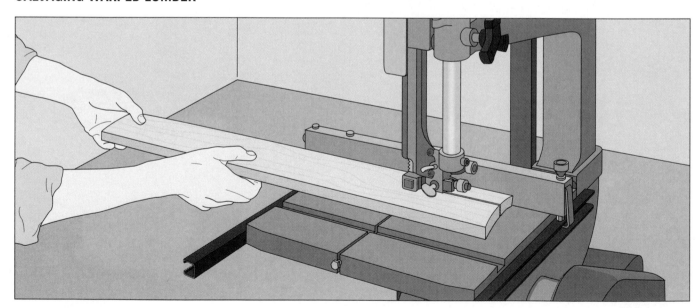

Ripping cupped stock into narrow boards

This technique for salvaging cupped boards involves the band saw, but you can achieve the same result with a table saw or a radial arm saw. If you are using a band saw, install your widest blade and set up a rip fence on the machine's table. Set the width of cut; the narrower the setting, the flatter the resulting boards. To make a cut, set the board convex (high) side up on the table and, butting the board against the fence, feed it steadily into the blade *(above)*. Make sure that neither hand is in line with the cutting edge. Finish the cut with a push stick. Remove any remaining high spots on the jointer *(page 55)*.

JOINTING CROOKED OR BOWED STOCK

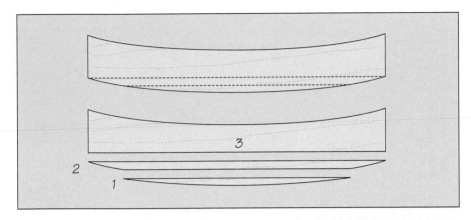

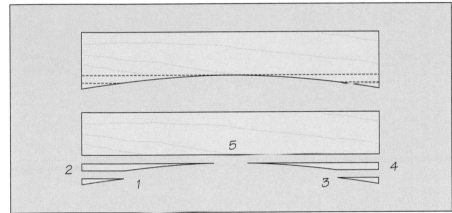

Jointing concave and convex surfaces

The diagrams at left show how to "straighten out" crooked boards on the jointer. The severity of the defects is greatly exaggerated for clarity in the illustration; extreme crook should be straightened on a table saw as shown below. On the jointer, the idea is to pass the high spot on the board's edge repeatedly across the cutterhead until the edge is straight. For the convex, or outward-bowing, edge *(left, above)*, pass the high spot at the middle of the board across the knives as many times as necessary *(cuts 1 and 2)*. Avoid "nose-diving," or allowing the leading edge to ride up during the cut. When the surface is flat, make a final pass along the entire edge *(cut 3)*. To flatten the concave, or inward-bowing, edge *(left, below)*, joint one end of the board as many times as necessary *(cuts 1 and 2)*, then turn the board around to repeat the process at the other end *(cuts 3 and 4)*. This operation is similar to basic jointing, except that you only cut the high spot at the trailing end of the board. Start the cut with the leading end of the board an inch or so above table level. Feed the piece toward the cutterhead with only the trailing end in contact with the infeed table. When the deepest part of the concave edge is above the knives, lower the leading end of the board onto the outfeed table and complete the pass. Once the surface is even, make a final pass the length of the board *(cut 5)*. Flattening bowed stock is similar to face jointing: with the board concave face down, make as many passes as necessary to remove the high spots near the ends. Use push blocks to keep your fingers safely away from the cutterhead.

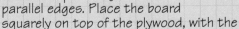

SHOP TIP

Straightening out an uneven edge
Even out the edges of a crooked board on the table saw with a shop-made jig. Cut a piece of ³⁄₄-inch plywood with perfectly parallel edges. Place the board squarely on top of the plywood, with the uneven part overhanging one edge. Butt stop blocks against the trailing end and edge of the board as shown, then screw the blocks to the plywood. Attach toggle clamps to the blocks and press the clamps down to secure the board to the jig. Set the width of cut equal to the width of the plywood piece and slide the jig across the saw table, cutting the edge of the board straight.

VENEERS AND MANUFACTURED BOARDS

Decorative matching of veneers can create unusual and breathtaking effects, such as the natural grain figure featured in this Victorian davenport.

The time-honored technique of veneering can transform a simple cabinet door into a flamboyant burst of color and grain, an unassuming piece of furniture into a seamless work of art. And though wood veneers have shifted in and out of favor over the centuries, woodworkers have used them to marvelous effect since the ancient Egyptians embellished objects with thin sheets of precious woods. In the 18th and early 19th Centuries, fine veneers became the hallmark of sophisticated, high-style furniture. Large swaths of distinctive wood veneers covered tabletops; marquetry pictures—delicate patterns made by aligning pieces of veneer and insetting them in the surrounding wood—decorated all manner of cabinetry.

Veneering declined with the advent of production machinery in the 19th Century, only to rebound once again in the early 20th Century with advances in manufactured board technology and improved adhesives. As materials continue to improve, veneering makes more sense than ever. Furniture that would be prohibitively expensive to craft from solid exotic woods can be veneered with the same woods at a much more reasonable cost.

And, of course, veneering today offers the same esthetic advantages it always has. With veneers, woodworkers are free to create stunning grain patterns with such techniques as bookmatching or slip-matching; they can arrange veneers in an array of appealing configurations—herringbone and reverse-diamond among others. They can also take full advantage of such beautiful but unstable wood cuts as crotch and burl, which are impossible to work with in solid form.

The old masters veneered over a solid-wood base, or substrate, using hot glue made from animal hides, blood and bones. They smoothed the veneer and pressed out air bubbles with special hammers. While hammer-veneering is still practiced, today's craftsmen may choose a more modern veneer press; they can also choose from a much wider selection of glues and substrates. The glue may be an aliphatic- or plastic-resin type; the substrate may be any one of a number of manufactured boards, most popularly plywood, particleboard or medium-density fiberboard. The introduction of these manufactured boards revolutionized furniture design: Because the boards are dimensionally stable—they neither swell nor shrink with seasonal changes in humidity—traditional frame-and-panel designs can be replaced by large unbroken veneered surfaces.

Of the variety of manufactured boards, cabinetmakers probably make the most use of plywood, itself a product of veneer construction. Plywood is available in many grades for many uses; always buy the best you can afford. Cabinet-grade hardwood plywood, which is already faced with attractive veneers, is a cost-effective alternative to solid wood—ideal for such projects as wall and floor cabinets, bookcases and drawer fronts.

Manufactured boards offer the solidity of hardwood along with greater dimensional stability. Clockwise from lower left is a sampling of the most popular cabinetmaking types: softwood plywood, medium-density fiberboard, particleboard, hardboard and Baltic birch plywood.

VENEERS

Veneer revolutionized furniture-making as far back as 2000 BC, when the Egyptians handsawed thin sheets of wood and then adhered them to thicker backings with animal glue and heated sandbags. Veneering soon developed into a refined art and became a hallmark of many furniture styles. The rococo styles of the Louis XV period in the mid-1700s fostered a demand for kingwood, tulipwood, purpleheart and rosewood veneers, while the Arts and Crafts movement of the late 1800s ignited a craze for marquetry based on mahogany, walnut and satinwood veneers. By the turn of the 20th Century, modern veneer mills served both the furniture and construction industries.

Almost as fragile as an eggshell and bursting with the warmth and opulence of exotic hardwoods, veneers are available in more than 200 varieties, some cut as thin as $1/100$ inch. Some of the most popular varieties are listed below.

A GALLERY OF COMMON DECORATIVE VENEERS

VENEER	COLOR AND FIGURE	CUTS AVAILABLE	SUPPLY	TEXTURE AND WORKABILITY
Avodiré	Golden yellow to gold; mottled figure	Quarter cut	Plentiful	Medium textured; easy to work. Stains unevenly
Black walnut	Light gray-brown to dark purple-brown; striped figure	Crotch, butt, flat, quarter cut, burl cut	Plentiful	Medium texture; grain difficult to work. Takes finish well
Brazilian rosewood	Chocolate to violet and black to brick-red; striped figure	Flat cut and quarter cut	Rare	Medium texture and oily; difficult to work. Resists finish
Carpathian elm	Brick red or greenish-brown to light tan; burl figure	Burl	Plentiful	Medium texture; easy to work. Takes finish well
Imbuia	Rich chocolate to olive-brown and gold; burl and striped figures	Burl, flat cut and rotary cut	Rare	Medium texture; easy to work. Takes finish well
Lacewood (Silky-oak)	Silvery pink to reddish-brown, fleck figure	Quarter cut, flat	Moderate	Medium texture; easy to work. Takes finish well
Mahogany	Light pink to reddish-brown, striped and fiddleback figures	Quarter cut, flat cut, crotch, butt	Plentiful	Coarse texture, difficult to work. Takes finish well
Maple	Creamy white sapwood with tan heartwood; curly and bird's-eye figures	Quarter cut, flat cut, crotch, rotary, burl	Plentiful	Fine texture; difficult to work. Takes finish well
Myrtle burl	Golden brown to yellowish-green; mottled and burl figures	Burl	Moderate	Fine texture; moderately difficult to work. Takes finish well
Olive ash burl	Creamy white with dark brown streaks; burl figure	Burl, stump	Rare	Coarse texture; easy to work. Takes finish well
Pearwood	Rosy cream; straight-grained figure, sometimes curly	Quarter cut, flat cut	Rare	Fine texture; easy to work. Takes finish well
Purpleheart (Amaranth)	Deep purple with light gray sapwood; striped figure	Quarter cut, flat cut	Plentiful	Coarse texture; hard to work. Takes finish well
Sapele	Reddish brown; mottled and ribbon stripe figures	Quarter cut	Moderate	Medium texture; easy to work. Takes finish well
Ceylon satinwood	Golden yellow; mottled figure	Flat cut, quarter cut	Rare	Fine texture; easy to work. Takes finish well
Yew	Warm orange with darker streaks; burl figure	Flat cut	Rare	Fine texture; easy to work. Takes finish well
Zebrawood	Cream background with dark brown lines; striped figure	Quarter cut	Rare	Medium texture; moderately difficult to work. Takes finish well

WHERE VENEERS ORIGINATE ON A TREE

Birds'-eye maple veneer

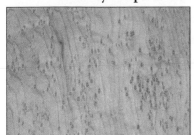

Figured veneer
Cut from irregularly grained logs;
produced by rotary cutting

East Indian rosewood veneer

Striped veneer
Cut across the growth rings
of trunk, accenting rays in
oak and striped and ribbon
figures in other hardwoods.
Produced by quarter cutting

European beech veneer

Flat-cut veneer
A tangentially cut veneer yielding
an attractive pattern of bold,
sweeping curves and ovals

Mahogany crotch veneer

Crotch veneer
Cut from the junction
where a tree trunk forks
into branches; features
a lush plumed pattern.

Carpathian elm burl veneer

Burl veneer
Cut from the end grain of irregular outgrowths and root sections;
commonly found in Carpathian
elm, madrone, myrtle, English oak,
walnut, ash and some exotic
hardwoods. Highly prized

Walnut butt veneer

Butt veneer
Cut from the stump, or butt,
of a tree; highly figured.
Produced by back cutting

Once its bark is stripped away, a log can be cut into veneer in one of three ways: saw cutting, rotary cutting or flat slicing. Saw cutting, which goes back to the early 19th Century, employs huge circular saws to rip strips of veneer from logs. Although not as efficient as other techniques, saw cutting is still used to produce some crotch veneers from irregularly grained or dense woods such as ebony.

Rotary cutting and flat slicing can produce veneers as thin as ⅛ to ¹⁄₁₂₀ inch and as long as 18 feet. In rotary cutting, a log mounted in a huge lathe rotates against a pressure bar while a razor-sharp knife peels off a continuous sheet of veneer the length of the log. Fir plywood, as well as some decorative veneers such as bird's-eye maple, are normally rotary cut. Half-round, rift and back cutting are variations that produce veneer from half-logs rather than whole ones.

In flat slicing, a half-log is held onto a frame that swings up and down against a stationary horizontal knife; a slice of veneer is removed with every down-stroke. Flat slicing produces crown-cut veneers. A type of flat slicing known as quarter-cut slicing is used on woods that display a striking figure when quarter-sawn, as in sapele, white oak or lacewood.

Flat-sliced sheets of veneer move along a conveyor for drying and storage in a veneer factory.

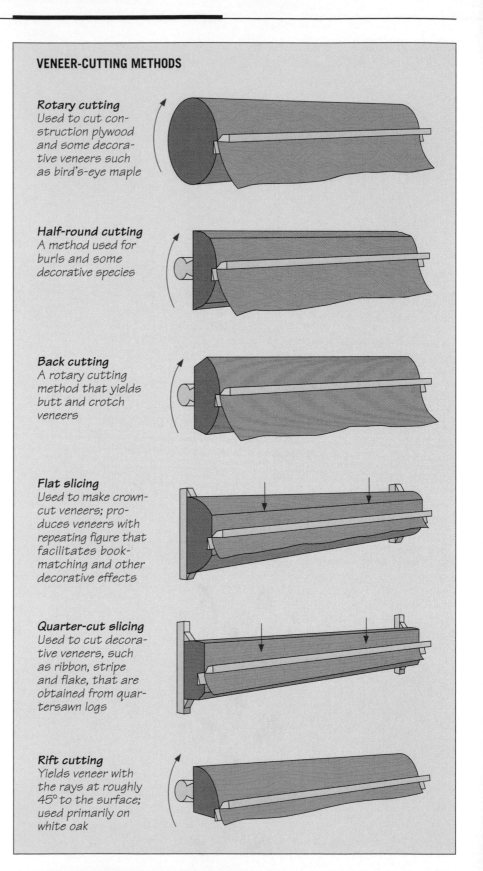

VENEER-CUTTING METHODS

Rotary cutting
Used to cut construction plywood and some decorative veneers such as bird's-eye maple

Half-round cutting
A method used for burls and some decorative species

Back cutting
A rotary cutting method that yields butt and crotch veneers

Flat slicing
Used to make crown-cut veneers; produces veneers with repeating figure that facilitates book-matching and other decorative effects

Quarter-cut slicing
Used to cut decorative veneers, such as ribbon, stripe and flake, that are obtained from quartersawn logs

Rift cutting
Yields veneer with the rays at roughly 45° to the surface; used primarily on white oak

VENEER TYPES AND SIZES

VENEER TYPE	SIZES	AVAILABLE SPECIES
Rotary cut	Length up to 10 feet; width from 8 to 36 inches	Bird's-eye maple, bubinga, Douglas-fir, masur birch
Flat-sliced	Length 3 to 16 feet; width from 4 to 24 inches	Ash, Brazilian rosewood, cherry, maple, oak, teak
Quarter-cut	Length 3 to 16 feet; width from 3 to 12 inches	Avodiré, mahogany, oak, Queensland maple, sapele, satinwood, zebrawood
Butt and stump	Irregular dimensions. Sheet sizes vary from 10 x 36 to 18 x 54 inches; average sheet size 12 x 36 inches	Maple, walnut
Crotch	Length from 18 to 54 inches; width from 10 to 24 inches; average sheet size 12 x 36 inches	Amburana, mahogany, walnut
Burl	Irregular dimensions. Sheet sizes vary from 8 x 10 to 18 x 54 inches; average sheet size 16 x 24 inches	Carpathian elm, English oak, madrone, myrtle, olive ash, redwood, thuya, walnut

SHOP-MADE VENEER

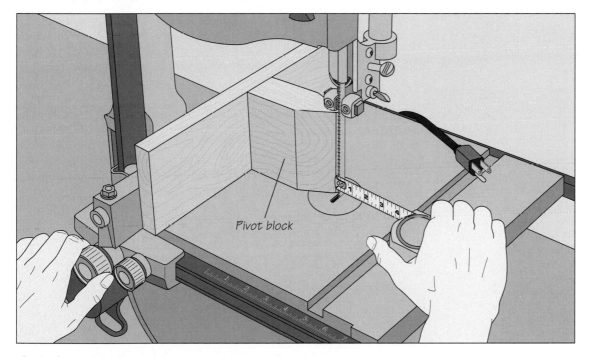

Pivot block

1 Setting up the cut
To cut veneer on the band saw, first make a pivot block from two pieces of wood joined in a T, with the outer end of the shorter piece trimmed to form a rounded nose. Install a ¾-inch resaw blade on the saw and install the rip fence on the table. Screw the pivot block to the fence so that the rounded tip is aligned with the blade. Position the fence for the width of veneer you want *(above)*, typically ⅛ inch. If the stock you are cutting is relatively thin, clamp a featherboard to the table to support it during the cut.

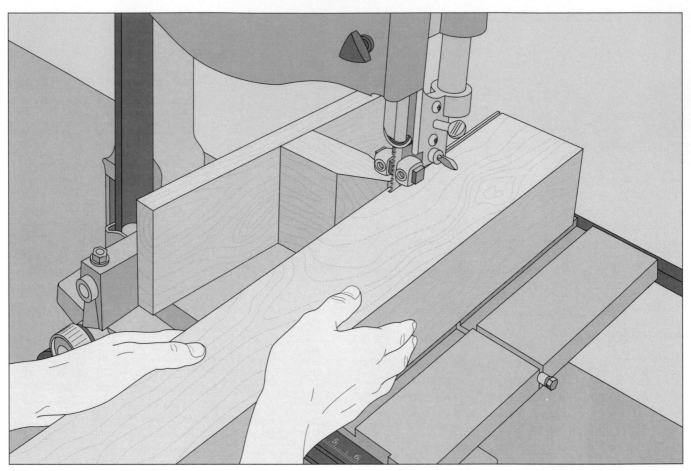

2 Cutting the veneer

Feed the workpiece into the blade with both hands, keeping the stock flush against the tip of the pivot block *(above)*. To prevent the blade from drifting off line, steer the trailing end of the workpiece. Near the end of the cut, move to the back of the table with the saw still running to finish the pass. Holding the stock square against the pivot block, pull it past the blade.

SHOP TIP

Salvaging warped veneer
Crotch and burl veneers sometimes become warped and brittle, the result of aging or improper storage. To flatten the sheets, dampen them using a sponge moistened with warm water and stack them on a piece of plywood with two or three sheets of newspaper between each slice. Place a heavy weight, such as a concrete block, on top. Let the veneers sit for a day or two. Wrap the sheets in plastic and store them under a weight until you need them.

VENEERING

Applying veneer is like woodworking in reverse. Instead of starting with a board, then cutting and sanding it down to its finished dimensions, veneered pieces are built up a layer at a time. Beginning with a substrate—or base—of solid wood or a manufactured panel, you glue banding to the edges and then wider pieces of veneer to both faces.

With a plywood base, orient the grain of the veneer so that it is perpendicular to the grain of the plywood, and both faces of the plywood must be veneered to prevent cupping. (Never apply veneer over fir plywood, because the grain of the fir can be seen through the veneer.) With a hardwood base, veneer should be applied parallel to the grain.

Furniture-quality particleboard and medium-density fiberboard also make good substrates for veneering. Since these materials have no grain (they are made of wood particles pressed together with an adhesive), you may arrange the veneer on the panels any way you wish. But the lack of a grain direction is also a disadvantage: Neither of these products is as strong as plywood, and any joints cut in

Specifically designed for cutting veneer, a veneer saw is usually used in tandem with a guide block or a straightedge to ensure straight cuts.

them must be reinforced with splines made of some other material.

Brittle veneers must be applied over a thicker underlay veneer such as poplar. Always cut the veneer larger than the actual size needed, allowing an overhang of about ½ inch all the way around. The overhang is trimmed off later.

If you are pressing down veneer the traditional way—with a veneer hammer—use hide glue, which is reheatable. Otherwise, white glue is your best choice. Whichever adhesive you employ, it will be effective only if the veneer is flat, clean and dry.

As shown in this section, veneer can also be pressed down in a veneer press. Newer commercial vacuum presses feature a pump that sucks the air out of a plastic bag that surrounds the substrate and veneer, allowing atmospheric pressure to hold the veneer in place.

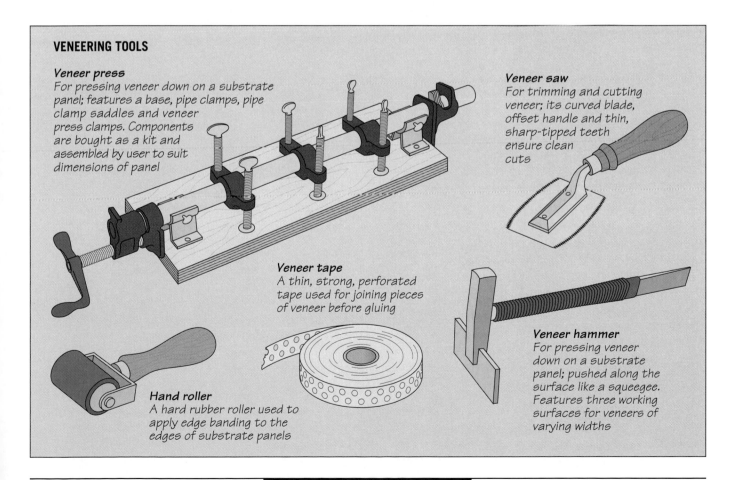

VENEERING TOOLS

Veneer press
For pressing veneer down on a substrate panel; features a base, pipe clamps, pipe clamp saddles and veneer press clamps. Components are bought as a kit and assembled by user to suit dimensions of panel

Veneer saw
For trimming and cutting veneer; its curved blade, offset handle and thin, sharp-tipped teeth ensure clean cuts

Veneer tape
A thin, strong, perforated tape used for joining pieces of veneer before gluing

Hand roller
A hard rubber roller used to apply edge banding to the edges of substrate panels

Veneer hammer
For pressing veneer down on a substrate panel; pushed along the surface like a squeegee. Features three working surfaces for veneers of varying widths

APPLYING VENEER

1 Gluing down edge banding

Cut four strips of banding for the edges of the substrate panel from the same veneer you will use for the faces. Make the strips overlap the panel edges by about ½ inch, and be sure their grain will run along the edges, rather than across them. Secure the panel in a vise, then apply a thin bead of glue to an edge. Use a small brush to spread the adhesive evenly, then center the banding over the edge. Lay a strip of wax paper over the banding and then, using wood pads to protect the edge and faces, clamp the banding down with three-way clamps, spacing them at 6- to 8-inch intervals, until the glue dries. Tighten each clamp in turn *(right)* until a thin glue bead squeezes out. Trim the excess banding *(step 2)*, then repeat for the other edges.

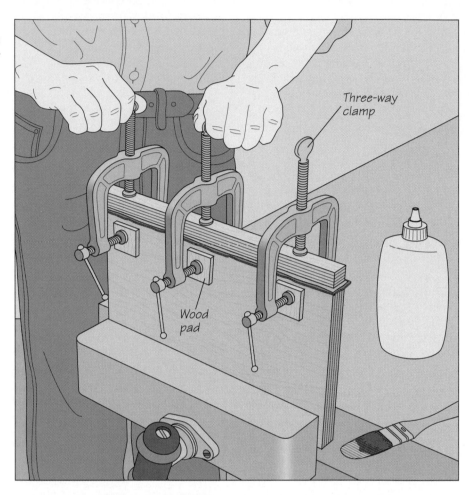

Three-way clamp

Wood pad

Veneer saw

2 Trimming excess banding

Once the glue has dried, hold the panel on edge on a work surface. Butt the back of a veneer saw against the far end of the panel with its teeth on the banding. Firmly draw the saw toward you to trim away the excess banding *(above)*. Make sure the back of the saw remains flush against the face of the panel throughout the cut. Turn the panel around and repeat on the other side. Excess banding can also be removed with a laminate trimmer *(page 68)*.

SHOP TIP

Cutting edge banding
To cut several strips of veneer edge banding in one operation, stack them one atop the other, edges aligned, between two pieces of ¼-inch plywood. Tack the two plywood pieces together with finishing nails placed along the edges; be sure the nail tips do not perforate the banding or pass through the bottom piece of plywood. Mark cutting lines for the banding on the top piece of plywood, then cut along the lines on a table saw or band saw. Be careful not to cut along the line of nails.

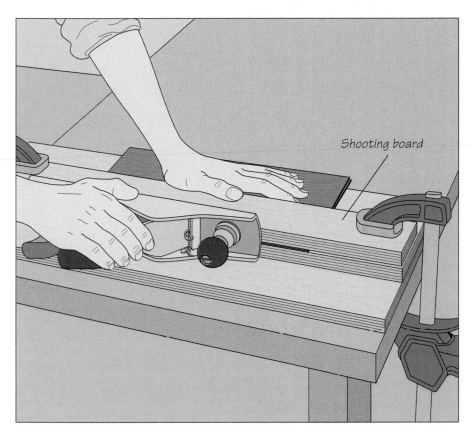

Shooting board

3 Edging the face veneer

The edges of adjoining sheets of veneer must be perfectly square if the two pieces are to butt together properly. To square them, you will need a shooting board. Cut three pieces of ¾-inch plywood slightly longer than the veneer. One piece should be wide enough to hold the other two pieces on top and the width of the plane lying on its side. Place the two pieces of veneer face to face and sandwich them between the top two plywood pieces so that the edges of the veneer are aligned and protrude by about ⅛ inch. Set the sandwich on top of the third, wider board and clamp the entire assembly to a work surface. Run the plane along the shooting board from one end to the other to trim off the projecting veneer. Make sure you keep the sole of the plane flush against the edges of the top plywood pieces during the cut *(left)*.

4 Taping veneer sheets together

If you are pressing down your veneer sheets with a veneer hammer, glue them in place individually *(step 5)*. If you are applying more than one sheet of veneer to a panel face and using a veneer press to hold them down, tape the sheets together and glue them down as a unit. Align the sheets edge-to-edge on a work surface, arranging them good-side up to produce a visually interesting pattern. If there are gaps between adjoining sheets, trim the edges on a shooting board. The combined length and width of the veneer should exceed the dimensions of the panel by about ½ inch. Once you have a satisfactory arrangement, moisten a few lengths of veneer tape with a water-dampened sponge. Tape the sheets together across their joints at 6- to 8-inch intervals, then apply a strip of tape along each joint *(right)*. Press the tape firmly in place with a hand roller.

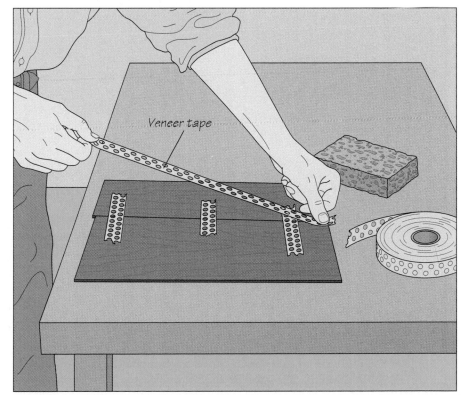

Veneer tape

BUILD IT YOURSELF

VENEER-TRIMMING JIG

Cut sheets of veneer to width quickly and accurately on a router table with the trimming jig shown at right. Refer to the illustration for suggested dimensions.

Cut the base of the jig from ¾-inch plywood and the top piece from hardwood. Choose a board with a slight bow for the top piece, if possible; applying clamping pressure near the ends of the board will flatten it, producing uniform pressure against the base. The top piece should be slightly longer than your veneer sheets and the base at least 12 inches longer. Screw wood blocks to the base so the top piece will fit snugly between them. Then screw a toggle clamp to each wood block.

To use the jig, install a flush-cutting bit with a bearing guide on a router, and mount the tool in a router table. Place the veneer to be trimmed between the base and top piece of the jig as you would when trimming with a shooting board *(page 65)*. Make sure the sheets protrude from the jig by ⅛ inch, then press the toggle clamps down on the top piece to secure the veneer sheets to the jig. Position the fence to set a cutting width of ⅛ inch. **(Caution: Guard and fence removed for clarity.)** Turn on the router and slide the jig across the table *(right, below)*, trimming the veneer flush with the edge of the jig. Be sure to keep the jig butted against the fence throughout the operation.

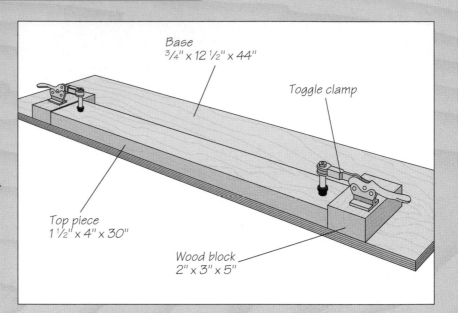

Base
¾" x 12 ½" x 44"

Toggle clamp

Top piece
1 ½" x 4" x 30"

Wood block
2" x 3" x 5"

5 Gluing down the veneer

Set the substrate panel face up on a work surface and spread on a thin layer of glue with a small brush or hand roller *(right)*. Do not apply adhesive directly to the veneer; glue will make it curl. Remember to use white glue if you are working with a veneer press *(step 6)*; choose hide glue if you are using a veneer hammer *(step 7)*. Handling the veneer gently, center the sheets over the panel. If you taped veneer sheets together, set them taped-side up. Make sure the veneer overhangs the edges of the panel evenly.

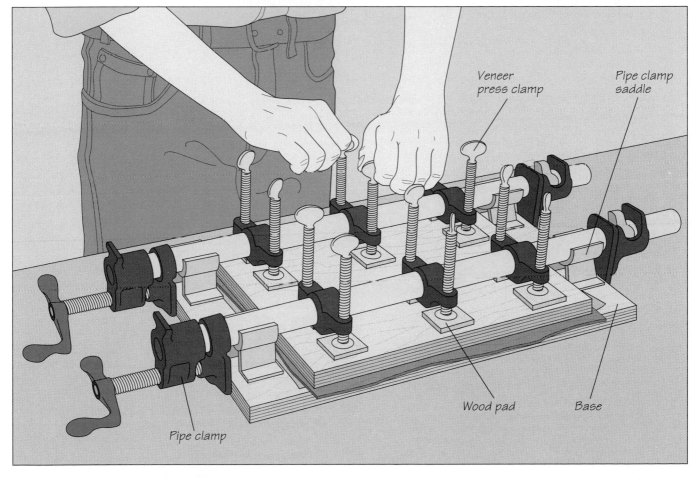

Veneer press clamp

Pipe clamp saddle

Wood pad

Base

Pipe clamp

6 Pressing the veneer in position with a veneer press

If you are using a veneer press, assemble the device following the manufacturer's instructions. Make sure the spacing between the pipe clamp saddles is slightly longer than the length of the panel. Set the panel on the base of the press, veneered face down with a strip of wax paper between the veneered face of the panel and the base. Protect the upper face of the panel with wood pads. Tighten the press clamps one at a time *(above)* until a thin glue bead squeezes out from under the panel.

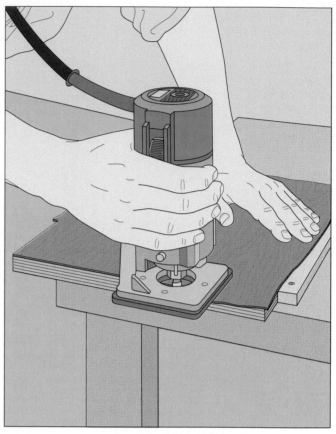

7 Pressing the veneer in position with a veneer hammer

If you are using a veneer hammer, set the glued panel veneered face up on a work surface. Butt wood scraps against the ends of the panel as stop blocks, then screw them in place. Holding the hammer with both hands, work the head of the tool back and forth over the veneer, pressing down firmly and following the grain. To eliminate bubbles or to smooth out sections that have not stuck properly, melt the glue by running a household iron over the veneer, then press down again with the hammer.

8 Trimming the excess

Once the glue has cured—2 hours is the typical waiting period—trim the veneer that projects beyond the face of the panel. Secure the panel veneered-face up on a work surface, positioning stop blocks as you would when using a veneer hammer *(step 7)*. Fit a laminate trimmer with a flush-cutting bit, then rest the machine on the panel with the bit just clear of the excess veneer. Holding the trimmer with one hand and steadying the panel with the other, turn on the tool and guide it from one end of the panel to the other *(left)*. Repeat for the other three edges of the panel. Lightly moisten any veneer tape and remove the strips with a scraper.

SHOP TIP

Veneering a curved surface
To press veneer down on a con-toured surface, such as the draw-er front shown here, use sand-bags or pillow-cases filled with sand. For best results, start laying the bags on the middle of the surface, working your way to the ends. Since moderate heat accelerates the glue-curing process, keep the bags near a heater as you prepare for the job.

DECORATIVE MATCHING

Since certain types of veneer, like some burls and exotic species, are available only in small sizes, producing a sheet of veneer sufficiently large for your project will often involve joining several smaller pieces together, with some cutting and taping before glue-up. Whenever veneers are joined, you must pay attention to grain, figure and texture to avoid cluttered or haphazard patterns. But as shown below, veneers carefully matched with decorative effects in mind can yield results unmatched by wood in its natural state.

Veneer sheets that are intended to be matched should be cut from the same log in successive passes. The result is a series of sheets that are essentially identical. The type of match you achieve depends on both the figure and grain orientation of the veneer and the size of the finished pattern you intend to create.

Artfully matching veneers can create eye-catching effects. This tabletop features a center diamond match.

Straight-grained woods, such as zebrawood and sapele, for example, yield veneers that are excellent for diamond, reverse-diamond and herringbone patterns. Burl, crotch and stump veneers can be butt-and-book-matched into large, elaborate circular and oval patterns ideal for creating interesting tabletops.

Recognizing grain patterns suitable for decorative matching takes practice. You have to know what to look for: A little swirl at the edge of a sheet, for example, may yield a beautiful design. To get a quick idea of what an end-to-end or a diamond match would look like, place a mirror at a right angle to the surface of the veneer; use two mirrors set at 90° to each other to preview a butt-and-book-match. Once you have settled on your pattern, stack the sheets of veneer so that their grain is aligned, tape the edges and cut the pieces for the match.

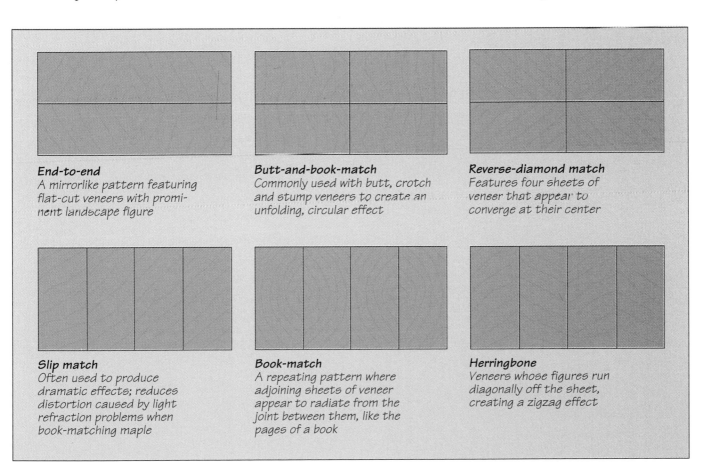

End-to-end
A mirrorlike pattern featuring flat-cut veneers with prominent landscape figure

Butt-and-book-match
Commonly used with butt, crotch and stump veneers to create an unfolding, circular effect

Reverse-diamond match
Features four sheets of veneer that appear to converge at their center

Slip match
Often used to produce dramatic effects; reduces distortion caused by light refraction problems when book-matching maple

Book-match
A repeating pattern where adjoining sheets of veneer appear to radiate from the joint between them, like the pages of a book

Herringbone
Veneers whose figures run diagonally off the sheet, creating a zigzag effect

PLYWOOD

Although it may not be as glamorous or as steeped in woodworking tradition as solid lumber, plywood offers several advantages to the cabinetmaker. First, it comes in a wide range of standard thicknesses and sizes. Second, it is dimensionally stable and is unlikely to warp or show signs of checking or splitting. Third, it is available with just about any commonly available veneer on its faces. And fourth, it is easy to cut. Indeed, plywood is a good choice for almost any design that does not involve intricate joinery such as dovetails.

Although veneer has a venerable history, and plywood is a relatively modern development—first produced commercially in the mid-1800s—the two are closely related. Plywood, after all, is a layered wood material made from thin sheets, or plies, of veneer. Decorative plywood is often faced with matched veneers made from high-grade hardwoods such as cherry or walnut. The veneer used in construction-grade plywood is peeled on a rotary lathe from eight-foot-long logs of poplar, pine or Douglas-fir.

As shown opposite, both decorative and construction-grade plywood are manufactured with an odd number of plies, giving the sheet a balanced construction. Three plies are usually the minimum number. Beneath the face and back veneers of a typical sheet are layers known as crossbands. The grain of each crossband runs at right angles to that of adjacent plies to counter wood movement. The result is a warp-resistant board that is equally strong across both dimensions. Some plywoods are also available with reinforced cores.

As with solid lumber, plywood is available in both hardwood and softwood varieties, although the terms refer strictly to the face and back veneers. Hardwood plywood is a stable and cost-effective alternative to solid wood, and is used in woodworking applications where appearance matters, such as for cabinets, drawer fronts and furniture. Softwood plywood is generally used for carcase construction, bookcases and shelving.

Not all plywoods are created alike. More than 70 wood species are used in its manufacture. Plywoods are grouped according to strength and durability; both softwood and hardwood varieties are available in four groups or categories that are usually stamped on the sheet. Group 1 (softwood) and Category A (hardwood) species are the strongest and most durable; Group 4 and Category D are the poorest grades. Refer to the chart *(below)* for the species that make-up the various groupings.

COMMON WOODS USED IN PLYWOOD CONSTRUCTION

SOFTWOOD

Group 1	Group 2	Group 3	Group 4
• American Beech	• Port Orford Cedar	• Red Alder	• Bigtooth Aspen
• Yellow Birch	• Cypress	• Paper Birch	• Quaking Aspen
• Douglas-fir	• Balsam Fir	• Alaska Cedar	• Basswood
• Western Larch	• Lauan	• Eastern Hemlock	• Red Cedar
• Sugar Maple	• Black Maple	• Bigleaf Maple	• Western Cedar
• Longleaf Pine	• Virginia Pine	• Jack Pine	• Cotton-wood
• Shortleaf Pine	• Yellow Poplar	• Ponderosa Pine	• Sugar Pine
• Southern Pine	• Black Spruce	• Redwood	• Balsam Poplar
• Tanoak	• Sitka Spruce	• White Spruce	

HARDWOOD

Category A	Category B	Category C	Category D
• White Ash	• Black Ash	• American Basswood	• Bigtooth Aspen
• Bubinga	• Avodiré	• Butternut	• Quaking Aspen
• Hickory	• Black Cherry	• American Chestnut	• Western Cedar
• Red Oak	• Rock Elm	• Hackberry	• Fuma
• White Oak	• African Mahogany	• Silver Maple	• Black Willow
• Pecan	• Honduras Mahogany	• Eastern White Pine	
• Rosewood	• Teak	• Western White Pine	
• Sapele	• Black Walnut	• Black Tupelo	

TYPES OF PLYWOOD

The basic design of all plywoods is the same: a core covered on both sides by layers of crossbanding and a face veneer. The most common type has a veneer core. All softwood plywoods are made this way, and they are stable, warp-resistant and inexpensive. Hardwood plywoods can also be made with solid lumber or particleboard cores. The middle ply of lumber-core plywood consists of several narrow strips of solid wood—usually mahogany, poplar or basswood—edge-glued together. Particleboard-core plywood has a solid core of particleboard or medium-density fiberboard. Lumber-core plywood holds nails and screws best and is preferable when additional strength and flatness are required.

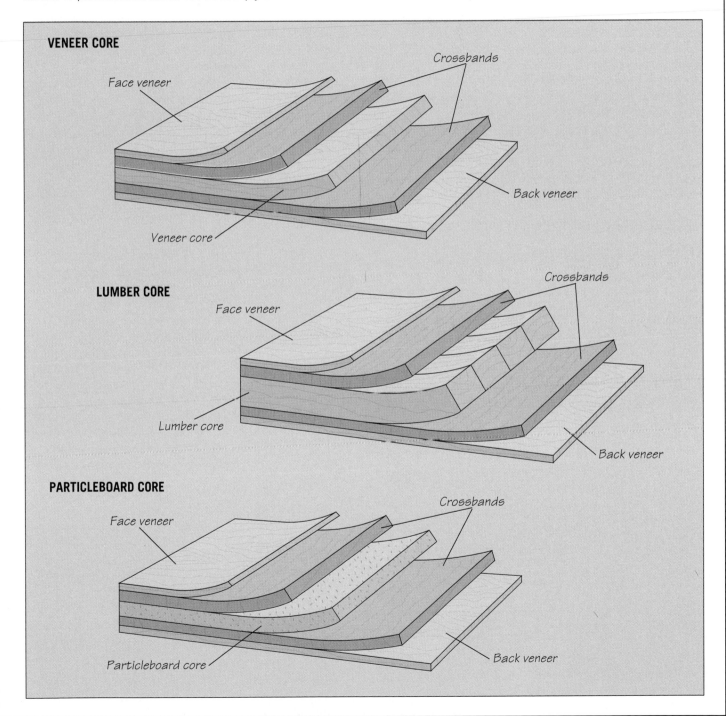

VENEER CORE

Face veneer

Crossbands

Back veneer

Veneer core

LUMBER CORE

Face veneer

Crossbands

Lumber core

Back veneer

PARTICLEBOARD CORE

Face veneer

Crossbands

Particleboard core

Back veneer

PLYWOOD GRADING

The wide array of plywood types available makes choosing the appropriate one for a project more involved than simply selecting a particular thickness. Both hardwood and softwood plywood panels are rated depending on how they should be used and on the appearance of their face and back veneers. They are also available in one of three grades, or durability ratings depending on the glues and veneers used in the construction of the panels. Softwood plywood comes in exterior and interior grades, and a category called Exposure 1.

Exterior-grade and Exposure 1 plywood are usually made with a waterproof adhesive, creating weatherproof panels that are resistant to moisture.

Their face and back veneers are cut from a relatively weather-resistant wood. Interior plywood is made with a water-resistant adhesive and is usually produced with an appearance-grade face veneer and a lesser-grade back veneer. For most interior applications, woodworkers generally choose Exposure 1 or interior-grade panels.

The three hardwood plywood grades are Types I, II and III. Type I includes fully waterproof exterior panels while Type II is an interior-grade plywood able to withstand some moisture; Type III is a moisture-resistant interior plywood. Types II and III are your best choices for most cabinetmaking projects.

The appearance of the face and back veneers is another factor that distin-guishes different plywood types. As shown in the chart opposite, both hardwood and softwood panels are available in six grades. If you are buying softwood plywood you can determine its grade, plus additional information about a particular sheet, by reading its grade stamp (below). Hardwood plywood is generally not stamped; if you need a particular grade, you have to ask for it and take the supplier's word that you are getting what you want.

Plywood is manufactured in a range of sizes. Softwood plywood ranges in thickness from ¼ to ¾ inch, while hardwood plywood is available from ⅛ to 1 inch thick. The standard panel size is 4 by 8 feet, but special orders can be placed for larger sheets.

DECIPHERING A SOFTWOOD PLYWOOD STAMP AND EDGEMARK

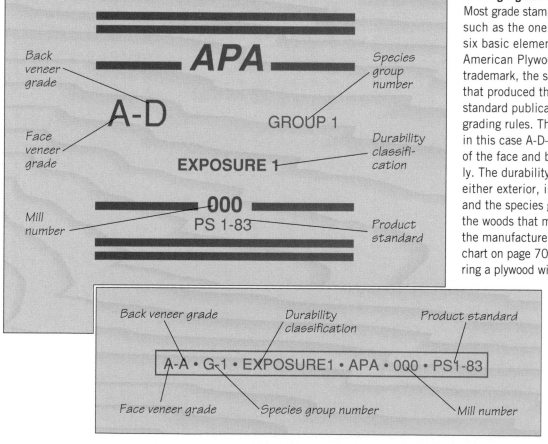

Back veneer grade

Face veneer grade

Mill number

APA

A-D

GROUP 1

EXPOSURE 1

000

PS 1-83

Species group number

Durability classification

Product standard

Back veneer grade

Durability classification

Product standard

A-A · G-1 · EXPOSURE1 · APA · 000 · PS1-83

Face veneer grade

Species group number

Mill number

Reading a grade stamp and edgemark
Most grade stamps on softwood plywood, such as the one shown at left, contain six basic elements. In addition to the American Plywood Association (APA) trademark, the stamp identifies the mill that produced the board and the product standard publication that contains the grading rules. The hyphenated letters—in this case A-D—designate the grades of the face and back veneers respectively. The durability classification may be either exterior, interior or Exposure 1, and the species group number indicates the woods that may have been used in the manufacture of the panel. (See the chart on page 70.) In order to avoid marring a plywood with two good faces—A-A grade, for example—an edgemark, such as the one shown at lower left, is used. Panel edges sometimes carry color stripes to designate the grade.

PLYWOOD FACE VENEER GRADES

HARDWOOD PLYWOOD	
Premium	Face veneer with well-matched seams and smooth; made of specific hardwood, such as walnut or mahogany. Free of contrasts in color and grain
Good	Face veneer similar to premium, but not as well matched. Free of sharp contrasts in color and grain
Sound	Face veneer smooth, but not matched for color or grain; defects only on back veneer. Generally intended for painting
Utility	Veneers have rough grain and may have knotholes up to ¾ inch, as well as some discoloration, staining and slight splits. Not matched for color or grain
Back	May have larger defects than utility grade, but none that impair panel strength. Not matched for color or grain
Specialty	Made to order to meet specific requirements, such as separate panels with matching grain patterns

SOFTWOOD PLYWOOD	
N	Sanded smooth; can take a clear finish; face veneer matched for grain and color, free of open defects
A	Sanded smooth; can take a natural finish, but is more often painted
B	Smooth and sanded; may have minor splits
C	Smooth; may have some broken grain, sanding defects and knotholes up to ¾ inch
C Plugged	Sanded; similar to C grade, but knotholes and splits are smaller
D	Used mainly for inner plies and back veneer; may have knot-holes up to 2½ inches

SHOP TIP

A plywood carrier
Sheets of plywood, particleboard or hardboard can be heavy and awkward to carry. The carrier shown here will make the load easier to bear. Rout a 1-inch-wide rabbet along one face of a 12-inch-long board. Cut a notch out of one end of a piece of plywood, then screw a wood block across the end of the notch to serve as a handle. Attach the other end of the plywood piece to the rabbeted face of the board. To use the carrier, simply hook it under the lower edge of the sheet and pull it up under your arm.

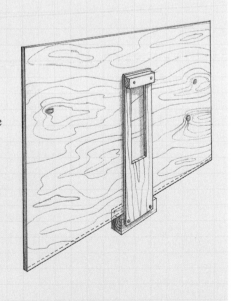

CONCEALING PLYWOOD EDGES

For all its advantages, plywood has one major drawback for cabinet-making: The multi-ply composition of the panels is clearly visible on their edges and ends. Fortunately, there are a number of simple options for concealing the unsightly plies. Pressure-sensitive wood-grain tape, for example, can be pressed in place by hand. Or, as shown below, self-adhesive edge banding can be applied with an iron. Both products come in several standard widths and wood species.

The illustration at right shows several more involved edge treatment alternatives ideally suited to custom work. With the splined miter joint, for example, the mitered edges of two panels are glued together and reinforced with solid wood splines. The other methods involve cutting strips of hardwood banding or molding and bonding them to the edges of the panel. The steps for applying one of these types—tongue-and-groove edge molding—are shown on the following page.

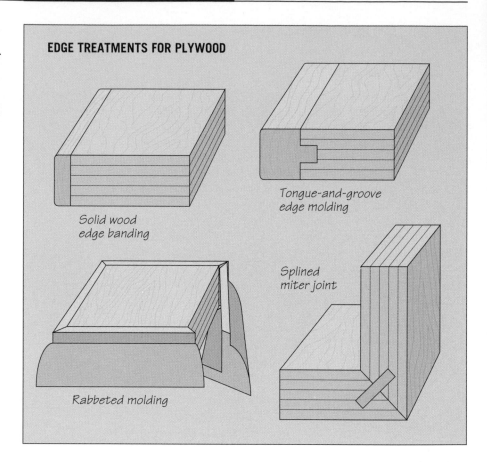

EDGE TREATMENTS FOR PLYWOOD

Solid wood edge banding

Tongue-and-groove edge molding

Rabbeted molding

Splined miter joint

SELF-ADHESIVE BANDING

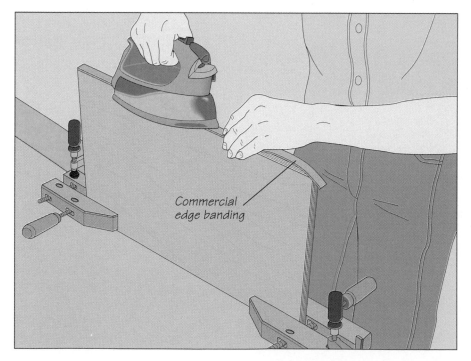

Commercial edge banding

Applying self-adhesive edge banding
Set a household iron on High (without steam) and allow it to heat up. Meanwhile, secure the panel on edge in a vise or with clamps, as shown, and cut a strip of banding slightly longer than the edge to be covered. Set the banding adhesive-side down on the panel edge. Holding the banding in place with one hand, run the iron slowly along the panel edge, pressing the trim flat. The heat of the iron will melt the glue and bond the banding to the panel. Keep the iron moving; resting it on one spot for more than a few seconds will leave scorch marks. Flatten out the banding by running a small hand roller back and forth along the length of the panel edge. Shave off any excess banding with a laminate trimmer (page 68).

TONGUE-AND-GROOVE EDGE MOLDING

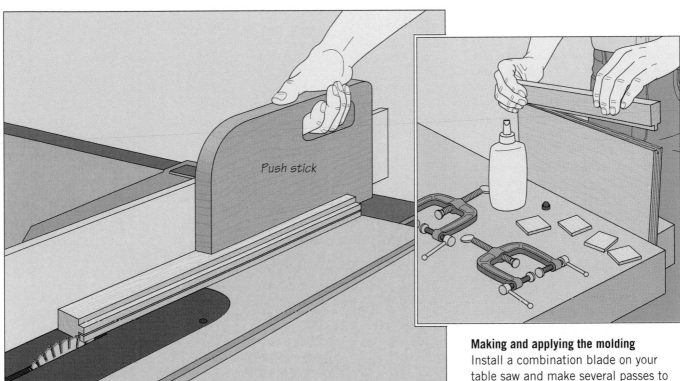

Push stick

Making and applying the molding

Install a combination blade on your table saw and make several passes to cut a groove one third as thick as the panel. Next, you need to cut the matching tongue; it should be sawn in the edge of a hardwood board the same thickness as the panel. Adjust the blade height so that it equals the amount of stock remaining on either side of the groove. Cut the waste from one side of the tongue, then turn the board over and repeat the procedure to complete the tongue; finish each pass with a push stick *(above, left)*. Cut the piece of molding from the board. Finish the job by securing the panel upright in a vise and spreading some glue in the groove and on the tongue. Fit the two pieces together *(inset)* and clamp them in place with three-way clamps.

SHOP TIP

Shop-made edge banding
Cut thin strips of edge banding from a board on the table saw. Make the strips slightly longer than the panel and at least as wide as the panel's thickness. Secure the panel upright in a vise, then apply a thin glue bead along its edge. Place the banding in place and tape it firmly at 2-inch intervals. When the glue is dry shave off any excess banding with a laminate trimmer *(page 68)*.

PARTICLEBOARD

Wood composites such as particleboard and fiberboard are a popular choice for carcase backs, drawer bottoms and concealed panels. Made from blends of wood particles and synthetic adhesive bonded together under intense heat and pressure, composite boards are as strong and as durable as most solid woods and generally less expensive. They are also more dimensionally stable.

Particleboard was first developed in the 1930s as a way of recycling wood flakes, chips and sawdust dismissed as sawmill waste. Today, many mills focus mainly on particleboard production, processing softwood and medium-density hardwoods into composite particles with machines called drum flakers, chippers and hammer mills.

Particleboard is manufactured by two methods: extrusion and mat-forming. In the less common extrusion process, wood particles and adhesives are forced together through a small, thin opening to form panels. The grain orientation of the particles is perpendicular to the faces of the panels. With mat-forming, the particles and adhesives are squeezed into a mat in a press. With this method, the grain of the fibers is parallel to the panel faces.

Mat-formed particleboard comes in three configurations *(right)*. Single-layer particleboard features wood particles of uniform size and shape. Multi-layer particleboard has coarser shavings at the core of the panel and finer ones on the outside surfaces. Graded-density particleboard is similar to multi-layer particleboard, but with a more gradual change from coarse to fine particles. Standard particleboard sheets are 4 by 8 feet, although 5-by-10 panels are available; thicknesses range from ¼ to 2 inches.

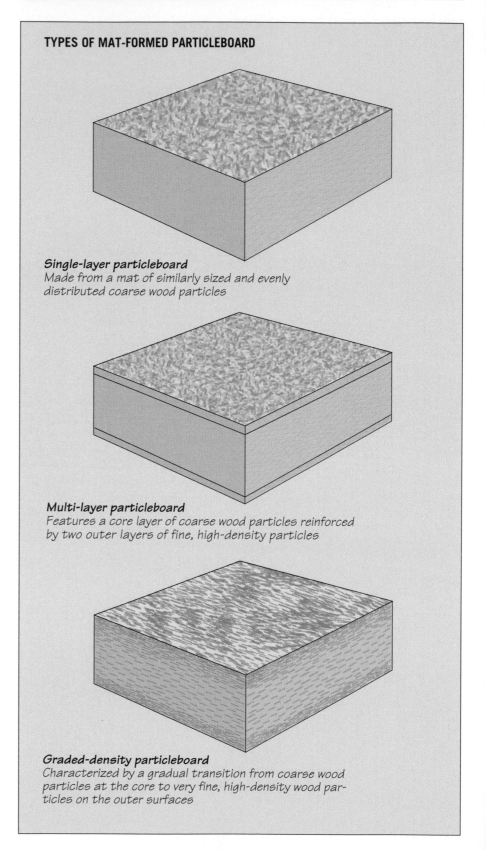

TYPES OF MAT-FORMED PARTICLEBOARD

Single-layer particleboard
Made from a mat of similarly sized and evenly distributed coarse wood particles

Multi-layer particleboard
Features a core layer of coarse wood particles reinforced by two outer layers of fine, high-density particles

Graded-density particleboard
Characterized by a gradual transition from coarse wood particles at the core to very fine, high-density wood particles on the outer surfaces

FIBERBOARD

Fiberboard, or hardboard, is pressed into mats much like particleboard, but because the wood particles are reduced to individual fibers, the result is a thin, hard and dense sheet with smooth surfaces. Hardboard comes in three grades: standard, tempered and service. Tempered hardboard is harder, heavier and more water-resistant than the two other types. Thicknesses range from $\frac{1}{12}$ to $\frac{5}{16}$ inch. Another variety, called medium-density fiberboard (MDF), features a fine surface texture with faces and edges almost as workable as solid wood. MDF is available in thicknesses from $\frac{1}{4}$ to $1\frac{1}{4}$ inch and can be bought with veneered surfaces.

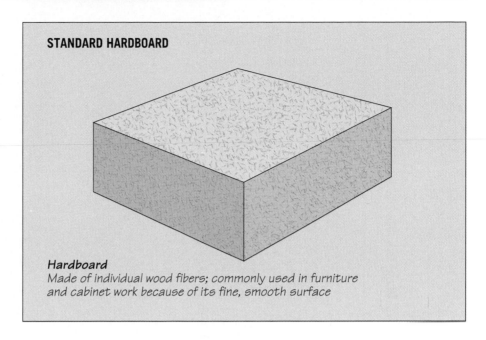

STANDARD HARDBOARD

Hardboard
Made of individual wood fibers; commonly used in furniture and cabinet work because of its fine, smooth surface

WORKING CHARACTERISTICS OF MANUFACTURED BOARDS

BOARD TYPE	WORKABILITY	FASTENING	VENEERING	FINISHING
Plywood	Easy to work; fine face veneers need little sanding	Face holds fasteners well, but edges often split. Bore pilot holes; screw diameter should not exceed one-quarter of panel thickness	Softwood plywood can be veneered	Premium and good grades of hardwood plywood need little finishing; sound grade can be painted; softwood plywood grades N and A can be painted or finished
Particleboard	Difficult to work; use of carbide tipped tools recommended; wear a dust mask when working	Hold on fasteners poor; bore pilot holes. Use finishing nails and drywall screws	Multi-layer and graded-density particleboard excellent for veneering	Multi-layer particleboard accepts most finishes; other types not suitable for painting or finishing.
Hardboard	Edges easy to rout, shape or groove; sanding of faces not required. Use of carbide tipped tools recommended	Face of tempered hardboard holds screws well. (other types not as well) Bore pilot holes and use sheet metal screws	Tempered hardboard can be veneered	Accepts most finishes
Medium-density fiberboard	Edges easy to rout, shape or groove; sanding of faces not required. Use of carbide tipped tools recommended	Hold on nails excellent; hold on screws poor	Can be covered with thin veneer	Can be finished or painted

DRYING AND STORING WOOD

A resistance moisture meter like the one shown above is a cylindrical device with two pins that are pressed into a board. The meter measures electrical resistance, which will vary depending on the amount of water in the wood.

Wood is by nature a hygroscopic material: It absorbs and releases moisture depending on the humidity of the air around it. As wood soaks up moisture, it swells; when it expels moisture, the wood shrinks. These simple truths have significant impact on every piece of furniture you build. For example, your joinery methods should allow for wood movement. If they do not, pieces of furniture can literally self-destruct. While the application of a wood finish may slow dimensional change, nothing can stop it.

Freshly cut lumber, or green wood, has a relatively high moisture content, which for hardwoods can range from 60 percent to 100 percent of the dry weight. This chapter focuses on ways of reducing that to a level suitable for cabinetmaking, around 8 to 10 percent, depending on the climate and species.

Unless you buy green wood with the intention of drying it yourself, your lumber is already either air-dried or kiln-dried. Air-dried wood may have up to 25 percent moisture content. Kiln-dried lumber has a lower level, 6 to 8 percent. Although kiln-dried wood is generally preferable for furniture building, some purists avoid it, contending that the process subdues the natural colors of certain woods and, in the short term, can induce internal stresses in the wood, making it difficult to resaw.

Large industrial kilns house hundreds of planks at a time, but there are a number of do-it-yourself models that are relatively simple to built, including a small-scale solar-powered kiln that will enable you to dry green lumber in your backyard *(page 84)*.

Air-drying wood is an equally worthwhile option for seasoning certain species of green lumber, provided the wood is properly stacked, stickered and covered. Stickers are small boards that separate layers of lumber in a pile, allowing air circulation around the individual planks. For a species like Eastern white pine, air-drying to a 10 to 12 percent moisture level is sufficient for most furniture projects. Whichever drying method you choose, you can use a special meter like the one shown in the photo above to measure moisture content.

Apart from control over the wood, the principal benefit of drying lumber in the shop is economic. The fewer operations performed on a plank before you buy it—such as drying and surfacing—the less it costs. For large quantities of lumber—say, 1,000 board feet or more—the savings can add up to hundreds of dollars.

Proper storage is as important as drying. Dried wood exposed to the elements can re-absorb some of the moisture that was extracted from it. There are several ways to store wood, depending on the kind of space you have and the wood you work with—from long planks to short stock too precious to be consigned to the kindling box. You can design your own lumber rack, using the ones shown in this chapter as starting points, or install a commercial lumber rack. If you use your basement to store wood, consider installing a dehumidifier to reduce the high relative humidity level common in such an area.

Kilns provide a fast and effective way of drying wood to a moisture level appropriate for cabinetmaking. Here, stacks of hardwood planks are loaded by forklift into an industrial kiln.

WATER AND WOOD

How wet is wood? This freshly cut log of Eastern hemlock contains 1.5 gallons of water or sap. Completely dry, the log would weigh one-half as much as its green weight.

As the moisture content of a plain-sawn plank of 2-by-10 softwood lumber drops below the fiber saturation point (FSP), the wood shrinks across the grain. At 17 percent, the board is ¼ inch narrower than it was at its FSP. It loses another ¼ inch of width when kiln-dried to an 8 percent level. Shrinkage depends partly on a species' density; generally, denser woods shrink and swell more than lighter ones. Sapwood also tends to change dimensions more quickly than heartwood.

Moisture changes in wood can cause problems for a piece of furniture, some merely annoying, others quite serious. A freshly cut log can contain water equal to twice its dry weight; made into a piece of furniture, it can turn stone dry. This capacity to hold different amounts of moisture under different conditions causes wood to swell and contract. If this property is not considered by the cabinetmaker, a drawer that opens smoothly in the dead of winter can swell and jam shut in the humidity of summer. A perfectly square carcase cabinet can pull itself apart as humidity levels change from season to season.

The amount of water in a piece of wood is often expressed as a percentage of its oven-dry or water-free weight. For example, if a 50-pound block of wood drops to 30 pounds after oven-drying, the weight of the shed water—20 pounds—divided by the wood's dry weight—30 pounds—is the moisture content of the original piece: in this case, 66 percent.

Wood holds moisture in two ways: as free water in cell cavities and as bound water in cell walls. As wood dries, free water is expelled first. When this is all discharged, the wood reaches what is termed its fiber saturation point (FSP). At this point, the cell cavities are empty, but the bound water remains, permeating the cell walls. For most woods, the FSP occurs between 23 percent and 30 percent moisture content depending on the species, with 28 percent the average. The key point to remember is that at the fiber saturation point, there is no dimensional change in wood from its freshly cut size. It simply weighs less. However,

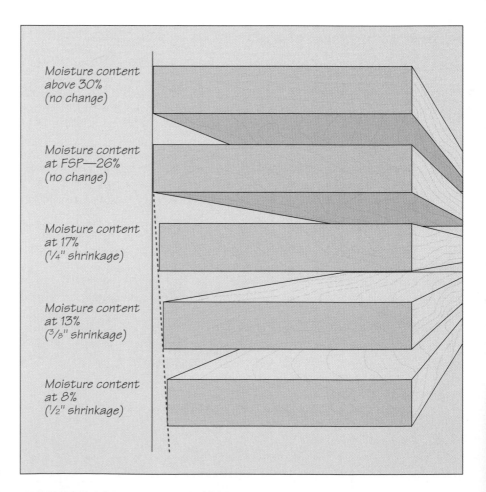

Moisture content above 30% (no change)

Moisture content at FSP—26% (no change)

Moisture content at 17% (¼" shrinkage)

Moisture content at 13% (³/₈" shrinkage)

Moisture content at 8% (½" shrinkage)

if the wood dries further, falling below the FSP, it loses bound water from its cell walls. The cells shrink and so does the wood. As the illustration on page 80 shows, the more bound water a board loses the more it shrinks.

The only way to prevent wood from shrinking is to treat it with a chemical such as PEG-1400. (PEG is an abbreviation of polyethylene glycol; 1400 is the chemical's molecular weight.) PEG-1400 diffuses into the wood and replaces the bound water, keeping the cell walls fully swollen. The treatment is suitable only for green wood, however, and is most popular for use with turning and carving blocks.

Wood gains and loses moisture as the relative humidity in the air around it changes. If the relative humidity rose to 100 percent, a piece of wood would reach its fiber saturation point and be at the same size as when it was milled. If relative humidity fell to 0 percent the wood's moisture content would drop to 0 percent. Because relative humidity falls between those extremes only a portion of the bound water is lost. Realistically, the moisture content range of most stock is 5 to 20 percent.

From season to season, the relative humidity in a given location can vary 80 percent or more. This is because relative humidity and temperature are closely intertwined. Warm air can hold more moisture than cold air. As a result, when cold winter air is heated, as it is in homes and workshops, its ability to hold moisture increases dramatically. If there is no added moisture available, the relative humidity plummets to extremely low levels. In contrast, hot summer air can hold a large amount of moisture. But when cooled indoors, it can hold much less. The result can be fairly high relative humidity. Both extremes cause changes in the moisture level of wood and in its size.

You can take several precautions to counteract the effects of changing humidity levels. If you store lumber indoors, try to keep the relative humidity fairly constant, using a dehumidier, for example, when the levels get too high. And although you may not be able to control the environment where your furniture will end up, you should build the piece to compensate for wood movement. When cutting a panel for a frame, for instance, leave a ¼-inch gap in the grooves that will house the panel. The extra space will allow the panel to expand and contract as humidity levels rise and fall.

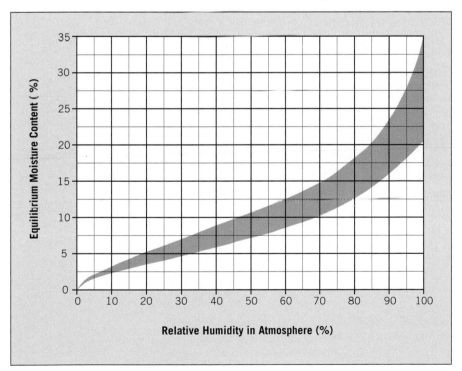

Relating a wood's equilibrium moisture content to relative humidity
Whether wood is in the form of a log, a kiln-dried board or a finished piece of furniture, its moisture content varies with the relative humidity of the air around it. As humidity rises, so does the wood's moisture content, expressed in percent in the graph shown at left. The moisture level of a piece of wood eventually reaches its equilibrium moisture content (EMC) after the humidity stabilizes. The EMC also varies depending on the temperature. The band shown in the graph covers EMC values for most woods at 70 degrees Fahrenheit. Those values decrease slightly at higher temperatures and increase marginally with cooling.

WOOD SHRINKAGE

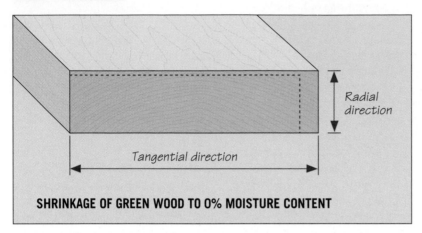

Radial direction

Tangential direction

SHRINKAGE OF GREEN WOOD TO 0% MOISTURE CONTENT

Tangential and radial shrinkage
Lumber does not contract uniformly; as shown by the dotted red lines in the illustration at left, tangential shrinkage—parallel to the growth rings—is about twice the radial shrinkage, which occurs across the rings. This difference accounts for the warping of boards and panels as wood expands and contracts with fluctuations in moisture content. Shrinkage along the length of a board is usually negligible. A 2-by-10 plank that shrinks ½ inch in width, for example, might lose less than 1/16 inch along its 8-foot length.

SHRINKAGE VALUES OF DIFFERENT WOOD SPECIES

Finding dimensionally stable wood
The chart at right shows the typical amount of shrinkage of various species in both the tangential and radial directions when green wood is dried to zero moisture content. (Values are shown in percent; a 10 percent value in the tangential column, for example, means that a 10-inch-wide board would shrink by that amount to 9 inches wide.) Although tangential shrinkage exceeds radial contraction in every case, no two species shrink by the same amount. The average is 8 percent tangentially and 4 percent radially. The key column of the chart is the third: The T/R ratio indicates the proportion of tangential to radial shrinkage. The lower the ratio, the less the differential between the two types of shrinkage and the more stable the wood. Species with relatively low ratios, like mahogany (1.4) and teak (1.8), are less susceptible to warping than woods with higher ratios, such as beech (2.2).

SPECIES	TANGENTIAL (%)	RADIAL (%)	T/R RATIO
Ash, White	7.8	4.9	1.6
Basswood, American	9.3	6.6	1.4
Beech, American	11.9	5.5	2.2
Butternut	6.4	3.4	1.9
Catalpa	4.9	2.5	2.0
Cedar, Alaska yellow	6.0	2.8	2.1
Cedar, Western red	5.0	2.4	2.1
Cherry, black	7.1	3.7	1.9
Douglas-fir	7.8	5.0	1.6
Elm, American	9.5	4.2	2.3
Hackberry	8.9	4.8	1.9
Hickory, shagbark	10.5	7.0	1.5
Holly, American	9.9	4.8	2.1
Madrone	12.4	5.6	2.2
Mahogany, Honduras	5.1	3.7	1.4
Maple, sugar	9.9	4.8	2.1
Oak, red	8.6	4.0	2.1
Oak, white	10.5	5.6	1.9
Persimmon	11.2	7.9	1.4
Pine, Eastern white	6.1	2.1	2.9
Pine, ponderosa	6.2	3.9	1.6
Sassafras	6.2	4.0	1.6
Sycamore, American	8.4	5.0	1.7
Teak	4.0	2.2	1.8
Walnut, black	7.8	5.5	1.4
Willow, black	8.7	3.3	2.6

MEASURING THE MOISTURE CONTENT IN WOOD

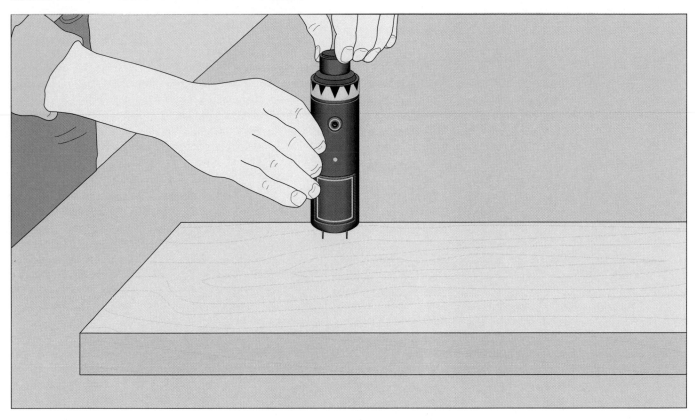

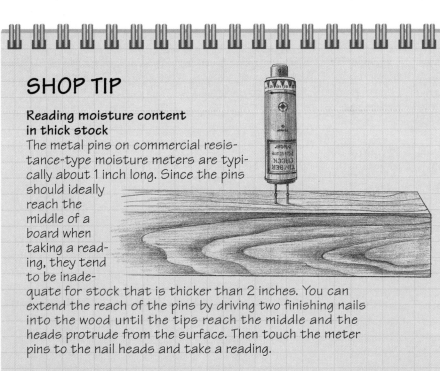

SHOP TIP

Reading moisture content in thick stock

The metal pins on commercial resistance-type moisture meters are typically about 1 inch long. Since the pins should ideally reach the middle of a board when taking a reading, they tend to be inadequate for stock that is thicker than 2 inches. You can extend the reach of the pins by driving two finishing nails into the wood until the tips reach the middle and the heads protrude from the surface. Then touch the meter pins to the nail heads and take a reading.

Using a resistance-type moisture meter

To determine the moisture content of your stock, use a moisture meter. Set the stock on a work surface and push the metal pins on the end of the meter into the face of the board as far as they will go. Twist the dial on top of the barrel until the light turns on and take a reading *(above)*. Repeat at several points and average the results. Alternatively, crosscut the board 12 inches from either end and take a reading from the freshly cut end grain *(photo, page 79)*. Most meters are calibrated for wood at room temperature—about 68° F. Follow the manufacturer's instructions to adjust your results if you are working in temperatures significantly above or below this level.

BUILD IT YOURSELF

SOLAR KILN

The kiln shown below, with a roof and front wall of tempered glass, provides a natural drying cycle. During the day, warmed by sunlight, the wood dries; at night, the moisture in the wetter core of the stock migrates toward board surfaces, ensuring more even drying.

Build the kiln according to the amount of wood you plan to dry and the space you have available. If you are reusing glass parts, such as used patio doors or storm windows, you may wish to base the size of the kiln and its framing on the dimensions of the recycled material. The kiln shown below and opposite is 5 feet wide, 16 feet long and about 8 feet high.

Choose a sunny location for the kiln, then level the surface and spread gravel over it. Lay concrete blocks at 2- to 3-foot intervals as a foundation, then build a base frame of pressure-treated 4-by-4s on top of the blocks. The rest of the framing and rafters are constructed with 2-by-4 stock; the floor, walls and door are made of ¾-inch exterior-grade plywood.

Once the base frame is in place, nail the floor on top of it, then construct a stud wall frame for the front of the kiln. Cut the studs to length and nail a sole plate to their bottom

FRONT VIEW

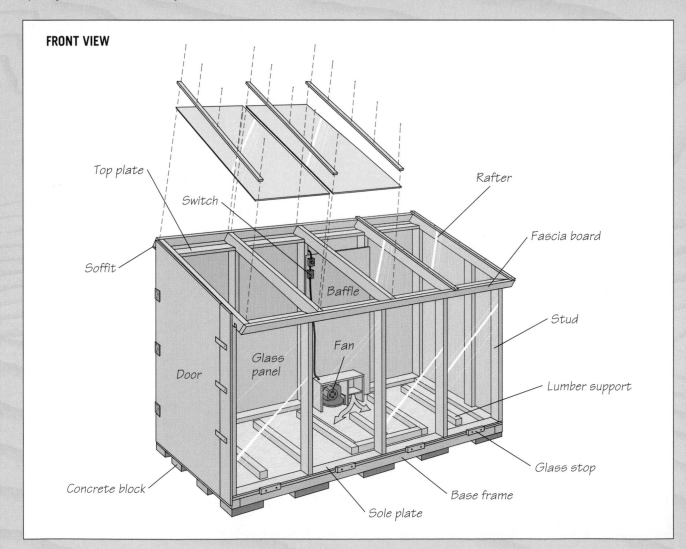

Top plate
Switch
Soffit
Baffle
Rafter
Fascia board
Stud
Glass panel
Fan
Door
Lumber support
Glass stop
Concrete block
Sole plate
Base frame

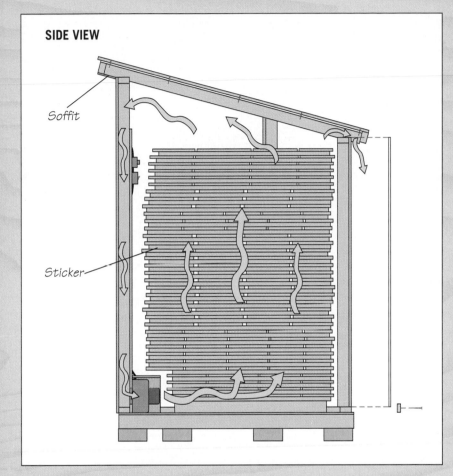

SIDE VIEW

Soffit

Sticker

ends and a top plate at their top ends. Recess the front edges of the studs about ¼ inch from the front edge of the plates to provide a ledge for the glass panels. Make the gap between the center of the studs equal to the width of the panels, spacing them no more than 4 feet apart. Set the wall frame upright and nail the sole plate to the floor and base frame. Repeat the procedure to make and attach wall frames for the back and sides of the kiln, this time without offsetting the studs from the plates. Cut the studs for the side walls so that the roof will have a 4-in-12 slope (4 inches of

rise for every 12 horizontal inches).

Cut the roof rafters to allow a few inches of overhang at the front and back, then nail the rafters to the top plates, spacing them to fit the glass panels to be installed on the roof. Tack fascia boards to both ends of the rafters, leaving a small lip above the top edges of the rafters to hold the roof panels. Cover the opening between the fascia and the back wall with a 1-by-4 board as a soffit. On the front of the kiln, this space should be left open. Next nail the walls to the outside edges of the studs on the back and one side, installing hinges and

hasp locks on one side wall to convert it into a door.

To install the glass panels on the roof, set them on adjacent rafters, leaving ample space between the panels for screws. Then fasten down 1-by-3 wood strips that overlap the edges of the panels to hold them in place. To accommodate the glass panels in the front wall of the kiln, cut notches in the bottom edges of the rafters, then slide the panels up into the notch, resting the bottom of the panels on the sole plate ledge. Screw 1-by-3 wood blocks to the front edge of the sole plate to support the middle of each glass panel.

To keep the air in the kiln circulating, fasten a piece of plywood as a baffle to two adjacent studs on the back wall, leaving an opening between the baffle and the top of the studs for air to enter. At floor level, construct a frame on the front of the baffle for an exhaust fan. The fan will pull warm air down through the baffle and circulate it through the kiln. Install the switch for the fan on the baffle, along with a thermostat to start the fan when the air temperature reaches 80°F and a timer to turn the fan off at night.

To keep the lumber stack off the floor, nail down 2-by-2 support pieces spaced about 16 inches apart. Pile the lumber as you would for air-drying, leaving adequate space between adjacent boards and separating the layers of stock with 1-by-2 stickers.

If you cannot supply electricity to the kiln, leave additional space between the boards to ensure adequate air circulation. Drying of the wood may take several months; use a moisture meter (page 83) to check on the lumber's moisture content periodically.

ESTIMATING WOOD MOVEMENT

Unless you plan to build all your furniture from manufactured boards such as particleboard and plywood, you should expect the wood you work with to swell and shrink slightly. This should not cause any problems as long as you compensate for the change of dimensions when you build your piece.

A good first step is to measure the moisture content of the lumber *(page 83)*. Then determine how much this moisture level will change as relative humidity fluctuates in the location where the finished piece of furniture will be placed *(page 81)*. Finally, try to estimate the amount of wood movement that will occur as a result of the wood's changing moisture content. As a rule of thumb, plain-sawn lumber will move 0.04 inch per foot of width for every percent change in its moisture content. The value for quartersawn wood is .025 inch. (The difference between the two gives a good indication of why cabinetmakers choose quartersawn over plain-sawn lumber when they want to limit wood movement.) If, for example, you use plain-sawn white pine with an equilibrium moisture content of 12 percent in summer which dries to an EMC of 8 percent in winter, you can count on as much as 0.16 inch of movement in width per foot between the two seasons. Changes in length are negligible enough to be discounted.

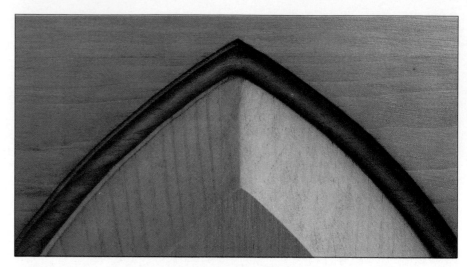

A thin line of unfinished wood is a telltale sign of wood movement in this closeup photograph of part of a frame-and-panel door. After the finish was applied, the humidity level in the room where the cabinet was stored gradually dropped, causing the wood to contract. A similar amount of movement in a carcase construction might have threatened the piece's structural integrity. The frame-and-panel design, however, allows for wood's natural swelling and shrinking. The panel floats inside a fixed frame with room for ½ inch of movement horizontally.

SHOP TIP

Making a moisture indicator
Keep this moisture gauge in your shop as a reminder of the relationship between humidity and wood movement. To make the gauge, cut a length of wood from the end of a glued-up panel, or bond a few wood blocks together edge-to-edge. Nail a metal pointer to one end of this arm, then attach the arm's other end to a piece of plywood. Drive a screw through the pivot hole of the pointer into the plywood so that the pointer is parallel to the end of the arm. Leave the screw loose enough to allow the pointer to pivot. As the relative humidity fluctuates and the arm swells or shrinks, the pointer will swivel to either side.

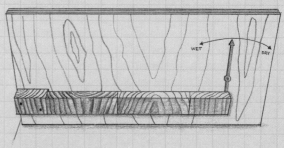

AIR-DRYING WOOD

The illustrations on page 88 show two simple ways to stack green lumber to ensure proper drying. As shown in the chart below, drying times vary for different woods. To avoid confusing different batches of wood, mark the ends of each board with the species and the date you stacked it. It is also a good idea to treat the ends of the boards with an impervious coating such as hot paraffin wax, varnish, diluted glue or a commercial end sealer. Otherwise, the ends of boards may dry more quickly than adjoining surfaces, causing checks to form in the wood. If you are working with logs, coating their ends will increase the amount of usable lumber the logs will yield by as much as 20 percent.

Whatever the size or location of your drying stack, air must circulate evenly around all the surfaces of the stock. This will ensure that the surfaces of the boards stay dry enough to pre-

vent fungi from causing blue stain. It will also help guarantee a minimal amount of warping of the boards. Placing stickers, or narrow strips of

Logs for carving can be stored in a pile one atop the other, provided their ends are not in contact. The ends should be coated with a sealer, however, soon after the logs are bucked to ensure even drying of the wood.

wood, between different layers of stock exposes the top and bottom surfaces of the boards to the same flow of air.

Lumber can be air-dried indoors or outdoors, but for best results, you should start the process outside or in an unheated building like a barn or garage. In a heated indoor location, where humidity is typically low and temperatures are high, green wood may dry too rapidly, which promotes checking. Outdoors, the lumber should be covered with a sheet of plywood to serve as protection from the elements. As the wood dries, check its moisture content periodically with a meter, keeping notes for future reference.

Wood destined for outdoor use need only be dried outside. For indoor furniture, the wood should complete its drying inside, preferably at a humidity level similar to that in the location where the furniture will eventually be used.

APPROXIMATE DRYING TIMES FOR VARIOUS WOODS

HARDWOODS	DAYS
Ash, white	60-200
Basswood, American	40-150
Beech, American	70-200
Butternut	60-200
Cherry, black	70-200
Elm, gray	50-150
Hickory	60-200
Maple, sugar	50-200
Oak, red	70-200
Sycamore, American	30-150
Walnut, black	70-200

SOFTWOODS	DAYS
Douglas-fir	20-200
Hemlock	60-200
Pine, Eastern white	60-200
Pine, sugar	15-200
Redwood	60-365
Spruce, red	30-120

These charts indicate the drying time for a stack of 1-inch-thick green boards outdoors. The low end of the range for each species is for lumber stacked in spring or summer—prime drying weather. The high end is for lumber stacked in autumn or winter. The figures assume that the lumber is dried in a region with a climate similar to that where the wood was cut.

TWO OPTIONS FOR AIR-DRYING LUMBER

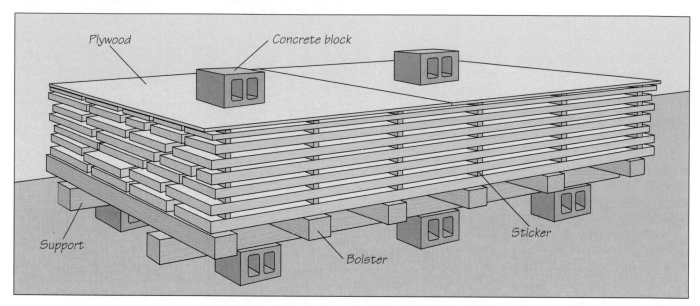

To air-dry a large quantity of lumber, start your stack with two 4-by-4 supports equal in length to the boards to be dried *(above)*. Rest the supports on concrete blocks. Then place 4-by-4 bolsters at 3-foot intervals across the supports. Begin stacking your lumber at right angles to the bolsters, leaving a space between each piece equal to the board thickness. Separate each layer with a 1-by-2 sticker as long as the width of the stack; cut the stickers from dry heartwood. Thinner stickers will slow the drying time for difficult species like white oak. Align the stickers with the bolsters; if you are drying thin stock, place the bolsters and stickers closer together to prevent the wood from warping. Cover the top row of stickers with plywood, topped with a pair of concrete blocks to apply uniform pressure on the stack and protect it from rain. Stack smaller quantities of lumber in support frames made from four pieces of 2-by-4 stock nailed together *(below)*. Build a frame for each end of the stack and one for every 3 feet of board length. The frames should be slightly wider and higher than the stack. Arrange the boards as you would for a larger stack, separating each layer with stickers. Space the stickers at 18-inch intervals, aligning one with each frame and also centering them between the frames. To keep the stack pressed down firmly, insert wedges tightly between the frames and the top row of stickers.

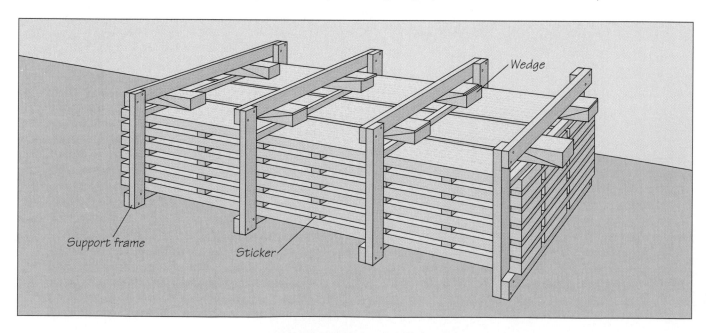

STORING WOOD

Whether you wish to store lumber, manufactured boards, dowels or "shorts"—all those odd-sized pieces you cannot afford to toss out—you should find a storage option to suit your needs on the pages that follow. The dimensions provided in the illustrations are given strictly as guidelines. Each design can be adapted to any situation.

The only design element you cannot skimp on is adequate support for the rack. A dozen 10-foot-long planks of ¾ white oak can weigh as much as 400 pounds. Rack supports should be secured directly to wall studs or to the joists above the ceiling at no more than 40-inch intervals. In most homes with 16-inch on-center framing, this means tying into every other stud or joist. If the walls and ceiling of your shop are finished, use a stud finder to locate these framing members. Some racks, like the cantilever type shown on page 91, may need footings, joist supports or both.

If space is at a premium in your workshop, you need to consider the design and placement of your wood storage system carefully. The end-loading type of rack used at most lumberyards is impractical for storing long stock in most home shops. You are far better off with a front-loading system, which makes it easier to load up new material and to shift wood around to find the particular plank you want. Avoid using triangular-shaped brackets to support lumber; they waste precious space.

Commercial lumber racks are available in various sizes and can be adjusted to different heights. The type shown can be screwed to a concrete wall or to wall studs. Four brackets will hold more than one ton of lumber.

SHOP TIP

Storing wood to preserve its moisture content

If you are in the middle of a project and have to leave it for a couple of weeks you may find problems once you return. A change in humidity—a sudden period of humid weather, for example—may cause the wood to swell or shrink. You can solve the problem by storing the wood in a plastic garbage bag or in vinyl, sealing any loose ends with tape. Wrapping the board will keep the moisture content of the wood constant, preventing any dimensional changes.

A TRIO OF LUMBER RACKS

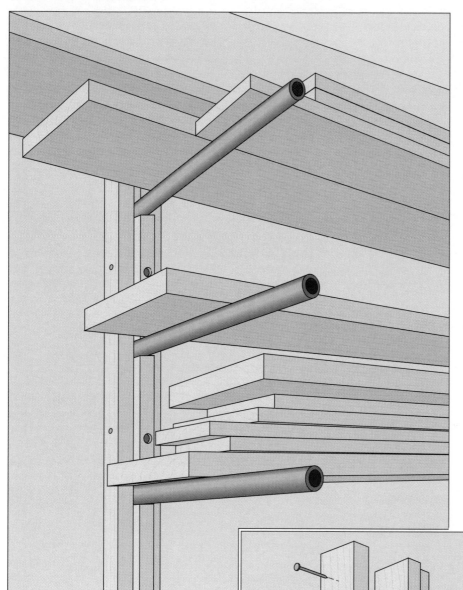

Building a pipe storage rack

The storage rack illustrated at left features three-piece vertical supports bolted to wall studs. The supports buttress the steel pipes, which carry the lumber. You will need one support at each end of the rack, with an additional one every 32 to 48 inches along the wall. Use 2-by-6 stock for the middle strips of the supports and 2-by-4s for the side pieces; the steel pipes should be roughly 20 inches long with a 1 inch internal diameter. Mark cutting lines on the edges of the middle strips at each point where you want to locate a pipe bracket. Make sure all the brackets in the same horizontal row will be at the same height. Saw the middle strips for the brackets, angling the cuts by about 3° above the horizontal so the pipes will tilt up slightly *(below)* to prevent the lumber from sliding off. Once all the middle strips are cut, nail on the side pieces, forming brackets with evenly spaced notches for the pipe supports. Bore pilot holes at 24-inch intervals into the wall studs and drill clearance holes through the supports for ⅜-inch lag bolts. Secure the vertical brackets to the studs with bolts that penetrate 2 inches into the wall, then slip the pipes into their notches.

Lag bolt

Steel pipe
1" x 20"

Side piece

Middle strip

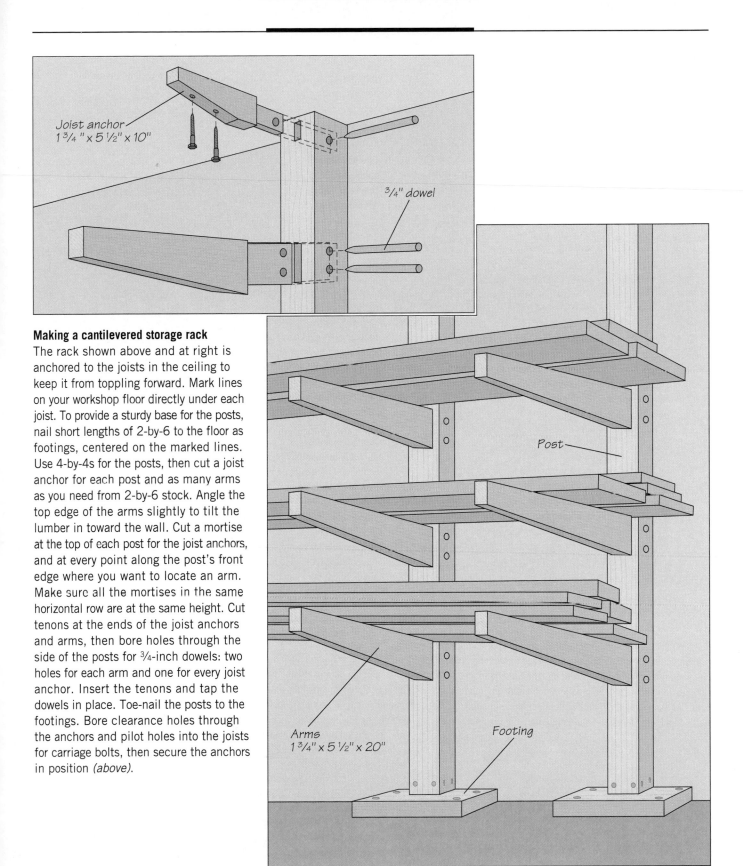

Joist anchor
1 3/4 " x 5 1/2" x 10"

3/4" dowel

Post

Arms
1 3/4" x 5 1/2" x 20"

Footing

Making a cantilevered storage rack

The rack shown above and at right is
anchored to the joists in the ceiling to
keep it from toppling forward. Mark lines
on your workshop floor directly under each
joist. To provide a sturdy base for the posts,
nail short lengths of 2-by-6 to the floor as
footings, centered on the marked lines.
Use 4-by-4s for the posts, then cut a joist
anchor for each post and as many arms
as you need from 2-by-6 stock. Angle the
top edge of the arms slightly to tilt the
lumber in toward the wall. Cut a mortise
at the top of each post for the joist anchors,
and at every point along the post's front
edge where you want to locate an arm.
Make sure all the mortises in the same
horizontal row are at the same height. Cut
tenons at the ends of the joist anchors
and arms, then bore holes through the
side of the posts for 3/4-inch dowels: two
holes for each arm and one for every joist
anchor. Insert the tenons and tap the
dowels in place. Toe-nail the posts to the
footings. Bore clearance holes through
the anchors and pilot holes into the joists
for carriage bolts, then secure the anchors
in position (above).

Fastening a lumber-and-plywood rack to an unfinished wall

The rack shown below, made entirely of 2-by-4 stock, is attached to exposed wall studs and ceiling joists. Lumber can be piled on the arms, while plywood is stacked on edge against the support brackets. You will need at least 8½ feet of free space at one end of the rack to be able to slide in plywood panels. Begin by cutting the triangular-shaped brackets and screwing them to the studs *(right)*. Cut the footings, slip them under the brackets and nail them to the shop floor. Next, saw the uprights to length and toe-nail their ends to the footings and the joists. Cut as many arms as you need, aligning the first row with the tapered end of the support brackets. Use carriage bolts to fasten the arms to the studs and uprights, making sure the arms in the same row are level. The rack in the illustration features arms spaced at 18-inch intervals.

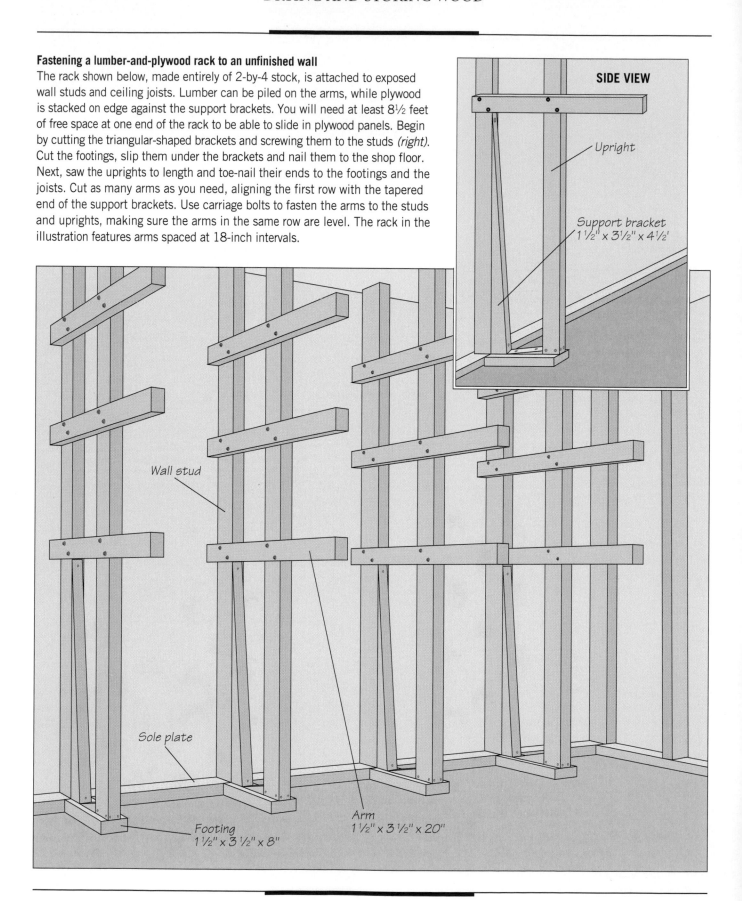

SIDE VIEW

Upright

Support bracket
1 ½" x 3½" x 4½'

Wall stud

Sole plate

Footing
1 ½" x 3 ½" x 8"

Arm
1 ½" x 3 ½" x 20"

PLYWOOD RACKS

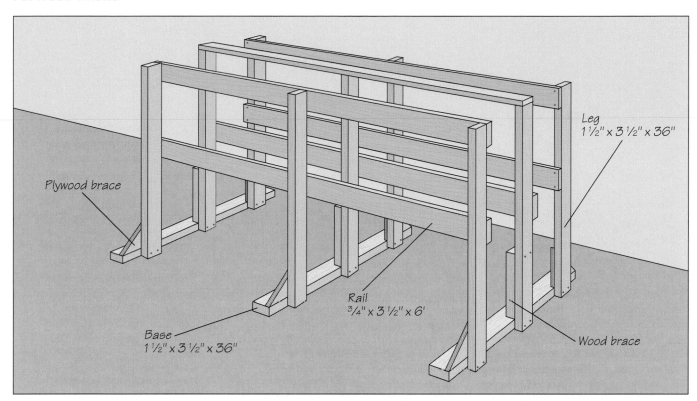

Plywood brace

Leg
1 ½" x 3 ½" x 36"

Rail
¾" x 3 ½" x 6'

Base
1 ½" x 3 ½" x 36"

Wood brace

Making a freestanding plywood rack
The rack shown above can hold ply-wood panels on edge without any wall support. Cut the bases and legs from 2-by-4 stock and nail the pieces together. To reinforce the rack, nail triangular braces of ½-inch plywood to the outside legs and the bases; use solid lumber braces to support the legs in the middle row. To connect the three sets of legs, cut rails from 1-by-4s and nail them in place: one halfway up the legs and another at the top of the legs. Set up the rack where you can slip the panels in and out end-first.

SHOP TIP

Holding plywood panels against a wall
Prevent plywood panels stacked on edge against a wall from falling over with some rope and a pair of window sash weights. Set two 20-inch-long 2-by-4s on the floor in front of the wall. Then screw two eye hooks into wall studs about 4 ½ feet above the floor. Cut two 3-foot lengths of rope, and tie one end of each to a hook and the other end to a weight wrapped in pipe insulation. Stand the panels on the 2-by-4s and lean them against the wall. Drape the weights over the plywood to keep them in place.

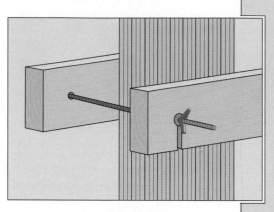

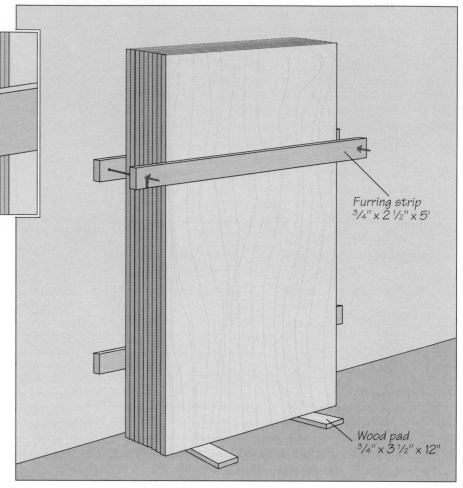

Furring strip
$^3/_4$" x 2 $^1/_2$" x 5'

Wood pad
$^3/_4$" x 3 $^1/_2$" x 12"

Building a vertical plywood rack

For long-term storage, stacking plywood on end not only keeps the panels from warping; it also saves precious shop floor space. The rack shown at right is built from furring strips, threaded rods and wing nuts. Start by screwing two furring strips to the studs of one wall, 2 and 5 feet from the floor. Then screw two rods 4½ feet apart into the top strip. Cut a third furring strip and bore a hole through it 2 inches from one end and saw a notch at an interval of 4½ feet. Both openings should be slightly larger than the diameter of the rods. Place two wood pads on the floor between the rods and stack the plywood sheets upright on them. Place the third furring strip across the face of the last panel, slipping one rod through the hole and the other into the slot. Slide washers and wing nuts onto the rods and tighten them, pulling the furring strip tightly against the plywood (inset). To remove a sheet from the stack, loosen the wing nuts and swing the furring strip down and out of the way.

SHOP TIP

A temporary plywood pallet
For short-term storage of a few sheets of plywood, make a pallet from four used car tires. Place a tire at each corner of a 4-by-8-foot area; stack the plywood sheets on top. The tires will keep the sheets level and elevated above any moisture on the floor. Do not stack anything on top of the sheets; the additional weight may cause them to bend.

STORING DOWELS

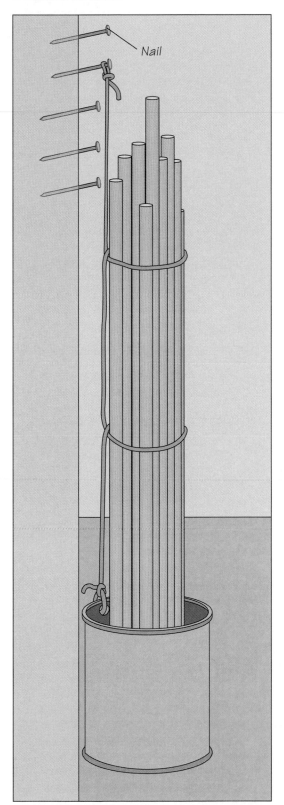

Nail

Wrapping dowels with rope

Dowels tend to roll around when they are stored flat. Stacking them upright is a better alternative, but then the problem is to keep them from sliding down or falling over. One answer is to loop them together with a length of rope, as shown at left. Drill a hole through a paint can just below the rim and tie one end of the rope to it; form a loop at the other end. Drive a column of nails, spaced a few inches apart, into a wall stud a few feet above the can. Stand the dowels in the can and loop the rope around them twice. Pull the cord tight and hook the looped end on one of the nails that allows the rope to hang taut. Move the loop up or down as the size of the dowel bundle changes.

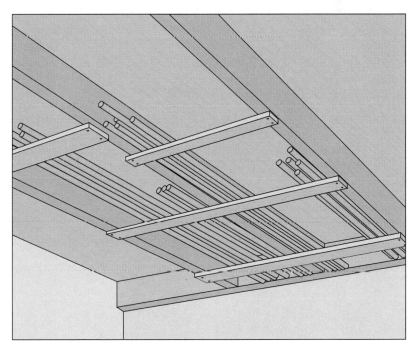

Storing dowels in the ceiling

The gaps between exposed joists in a shop ceiling are often considered wasted space, but you can make good use of them to hold dowels. Screw a couple of 1-by-3 furring strips across the bottom of the joists and then rest the stock on top of strips. This method is particularly useful for long dowels, which can clutter a workshop.

STORING SHORT STOCK

Constructing a rack with a mobile base

Sorting through a jumbled wood pile in a corner of the shop for a piece of short stock of the right size can be frustrating. The rack shown at right stores short pieces according to size. The bottom section is a box with dividers, ideal for storing pieces of plywood; the box is made with ¾-inch plywood, while the dividers are ¼-inch plywood. The top section, built from ¾-inch plywood, consists of a back panel, triangular-shaped sides and ¼" plywood shelves spaced according to the diameter of the containers you place between them. The rack shown features 5-gallon cans below the bottom shelf and plastic tubes of varying sizes on the other shelves. Keep short stock in the cans and tubing. Cut triangular cutouts near the top of the sides to hold dowels flat. To make the rack mobile, fasten it to a shop-built dolly with casters *(below)*. Cut a piece of plywood to the same dimensions as the base of the rack, then screw corner blocks to one side. Attach a heavy-duty caster to each corner block.

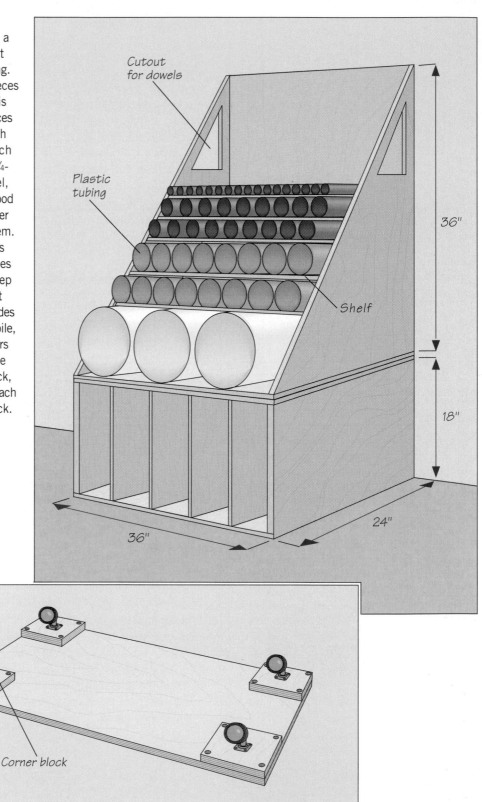

Cutout for dowels

Plastic tubing

Shelf

36"

18"

24"

36"

Corner block

Making a combination workbench and short-cut bin

In a workshop with limited space, build a work table with short-cut storage space underneath, such as the one shown at right. Cut 2-by-4s to length for the legs; support them with 2-by-4 braces—one set nailed a few inches above the floor and a second set attached flush with the top of the legs. Cut the top and two shelves from ¾" plywood, then nail them to the braces. Saw notches out of the corners of the shelves to fit around the legs. Make dividers from ¼ inch plywood and attach them between the shelves using quarter-round molding strips nailed into the shelves.

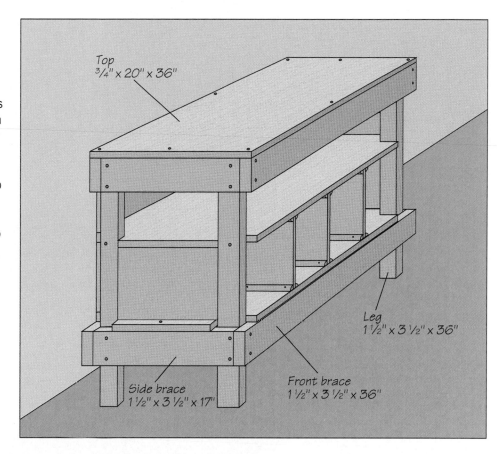

Top
¾" x 20" x 36"

Leg
1 ½" x 3 ½" x 36"

Side brace
1 ½" x 3 ½" x 17"

Front brace
1 ½" x 3 ½" x 36"

Spring clip

Dowel

Shelf

Stacking stock between wall studs

Store short stock between the studs of an unfinished shop wall. To keep the wood from falling over, screw spring clips to the studs and insert dowels into the clips to span the gaps between adjacent studs *(left)*. To stand shorter lengths of stock higher up on the wall, cut shelves and support cleats from scrap wood. Screw the cleats to the studs and rest the shelves on top of them.

WOOD DIRECTORY

Trees have formed a part of the Earth's landscape for more than 300 million years— since before dinosaurs first roamed the planet. In that time they have developed a remarkable diversity of species, numbering more than 1,000 varieties in the United States alone. Trees come in many sizes and shapes, from the stunted spruces of northern Canada to the sublime, towering stands of California's giant sequoias. Wood's diversity is also apparent in the wide array of colors and grain patterns available to the woodworker, from the bold vermilion hue of padauk and the inky blackness of ebony to the intricate, swirling designs of walnut burl.

The 78 species of wood shown in this directory were chosen with the needs and interests of the cabinetmaker foremost in mind. The basic cabinetmaking woods are here—species such as oak, pine, cherry and ash. But there are also a number of less familiar exotic woods too, from afrormosia to ziricote. Some you may have only read about; others you may be seeing for the first time. In either case, the photos and information may inspire you to new adventures in your upcoming woodworking projects.

The directory is arranged alphabetically according to a wood's most commonly used name. Sometimes a wood may be known by several names; to avoid confusion you may need to use the botanical name when buying a particular species ("spp." indicates that the wood comes from several species belonging to that genus). The woods in this chapter were photographed with a clear lacquer finish to highlight their color and figure. For this reason—and because of the inevitable variations within species—the unfinished wood that you buy may look somewhat different.

Hardwoods are indicated with an (H); softwoods with an (S). However, do not take the terms too literally. Some softwoods are actually harder than some hardwoods. For more information on the differences between the two groups, see page 24.

The workability category gives information about the ease or difficulty of working with a particular wood. Some species may be tough to plane unless you reduce the angle of the blade, while others may require you to pre-bore for nailing.

Rather than providing a specific cost per board foot—which can fluctuate—for each wood, price is listed on a relative scale, from inexpensive to expensive. Usually, the pricier woods are chosen for a special part of a piece of furniture. You might select a piece of cocobolo, for example, to make a drawer pull, or an inlay of ebony to add a decorative touch to a chair leg.

All the woods shown are commercially available in North America; for species you cannot find locally, check woodworking magazines for mail-order sources. However, some species are becoming increasingly rare, and a few tropical hardwoods are in danger of extinction. Trade in many species is severely restricted, and for this reason, woodworkers often must seek alternatives to using traditional woods. Fortunately, there are many, and their number is growing. Some have long been available: pau ferro, for example, which is strikingly similar to the costly, endangered Brazilian rosewood. Others—so-called "good woods," grown and harvested with a view to conservation and sustainable growth—are recent arrivals in North America. These lesser-known species, imported primarily from Central and South America at present, originate from sources that are monitored in order to be certified as well-managed. Four of these woods are featured in this directory: bayo, chactacote, chontaquiro amarillo and tornillo. (You can learn more about these woods and where to buy them through the Woodworkers Alliance for Rainforest Protection in Coos Bay, Oregon; the Rainforest Alliance in New York; or Scientific Certification Systems in Oakland, California.)

You may want to avoid the problems of scarcity by building your projects with more plentiful woods or plywood, then covering them with a beautiful veneer. Another alternative is recycled wood, scavenged from old buildings, shipping crates or pallets. With effort and imagination you can transform many workaday items into handsome pieces.

 This symbol indicates a species that is rare or endangered in at least one of the countries where it is harvested.

AFRORMOSIA
(H)

Botanical Name: *Pericopsis elata*

A dense, durable wood, afrormosia resembles teak in color and texture; like teak, it is also an endangered species. First marketed in the years following World War II for use in construction, afrormosia soon came to be valued for its decorative properties.

Other Names: Assamela (Ivory Coast, France); kokrodua (Ghana, Ivory Coast); ayin, egbi (Nigeria); devil's tree.

Source: West Africa.

Characteristics: Straight to interlocked grain; moderately fine texture; yellow-brown, darkens to a rich golden brown with exposure.

Uses: Indoor and outdoor furniture, boat building, cabinetmaking and decorative veneers.

Workability: Generally good with all woodworking tools; raise cutting angle when planing, as wood may tear out; moderate blunting of cutters; pre-bore for nailing; medium bending properties.

Finishing: Accepts finishes very well.

Weight: 43 lb./cu. ft.

Price: Expensive.

AGBA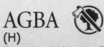
(H)

Botanical Name: *Gossweilerodendron balsamiferum*

One of Africa's largest trees, often growing to heights of 120 feet, agba is undoubtedly one of its most useful. Attractive, durable and lightweight, it resembles South American mahogany and has approximately the same strength. Occasional pieces may be extremely brittle or gummy, making it necessary to be especially careful when selecting this lumber.

Other Names: Tola (Zaire); tola branca, white tola (Angola); Nigerian cedar (U.K.); nitola (Congo); mutseka-mambole (Nigeria).

Source: Tropical West Africa.

Characteristics: Straight to somewhat interlocked grain; moderately fine texture; straw-brown, often with a pink tint.

Uses: Furniture, turning, plywood, boat building, moldings, paneling and occasionally for veneers.

Workability: Generally very good; slight blunting of cutters; low bending properties; gum in wood may cause saw blades to bind.

Finishing: Accepts finishes well when filled.

Weight: 32 lb./cu. ft.

Price: Moderate.

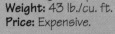

ALDER, RED
(H)

Botanical Name: *Alnus rubra*

Red alder is easy to cut and it takes finishes very well, especially if a wash coat of thinned shellac is applied before staining. This wood can be of significant value in woodworking, despite its relatively modest reputation. Even defective alder should not be pegged for firewood. Defects, such as burls and stains, can produce beautiful veneers.

Other Names: Western alder, Oregon alder.

Source: Pacific Coast of North America.

Characteristics: Generally straight grain; fine, even texture; pale yellow to reddish-brown.

Uses: Turning, furniture, carving, plywood and veneers.

Workability: Generally good; reduce blade angle when planing to prevent tearout; only slight blunting of cutters; low bending properties.

Finishing: Accepts finishes well.

Weight: 33 lb./cu. ft.

Price: Inexpensive.

AMBURANA
(H)

Botanical Name: *Amburana cearensis*

Relatively strong for its weight, amburana is a good choice for joinery. Its irregular orange rays produce attractive veneers. Found mainly in the tropical, dry regions of South America, the trees often tower to 100 feet. The wood can pique the senses with an odor of vanilla.

Other Names: Cerejeira, cumare, cumaru, rajada (Brazil); roble del pais, palo trebol (Argentina); ishpingo (Peru).

Sources: Central and South America.

Characteristics: Interlocked and irregular grain; medium to coarse texture; yellow to pale brown with a subtle orange tint, darkening slightly with exposure.

Uses: Furniture, joinery, boat building and veneers.

Workability: Good; dulls cutting edges moderately; reduce cutting angle of blade when planing irregular grain; pre-bore for nailing; moderate bending properties.

Finishing: Accepts finishes well when filled.

Weight: 37 lb./cu. ft.

Price: Moderate.

ASH, BLACK
(H)

Botanical Name: *Fraxinus nigra*

Often known as swamp or water ash, black ash grows mainly in the wetlands of eastern North America. As the softest American ash, it is more likely to be found in interior joinery and cabinetwork than in sports equipment, where white ash is commonly used. It also has a significant history as a weaving wood for many types of baskets. Black ash's rotary cut and sliced veneers are highly decorative and much sought after.

Other Names: Brown ash, hoop ash, swamp ash, water ash, northern brown ash.

Sources: U.S.A. and Canada.

Characteristics: Straight grain; coarse, even texture; dark, grayish brown.

Uses: Joinery, cabinetwork, plywood and veneers.

Workability: Generally good; blunts cutters moderately; excellent bending properties.

Finishing: Accepts finishes well.

Weight: 35 lb./cu. ft.

Price: Inexpensive.

ASH, WHITE
(H)

Botanical Name: *Fraxinus americana*

White ash can be considered the all-American leisure wood. Strong and very shock-resistant, it is used to make oars, pool cues and baseball bats. It is also the wood of choice for garden-tool handles, used extensively in boat building and cut into decorative veneers. It often has a highly variegated heartwood, known as olive ash or calico ash.

Other Names: American white ash, Canadian ash, American ash.

Sources: Canada and U.S.A.

Characteristics: Straight grain; coarse texture; light-brown heartwood with almost white sapwood.

Uses: Baseball bats, pool cues, oars, tool handles, boat building, furniture and veneers.

Workability: Satisfactory; moderate blunting of cutters; excellent bending properties; pre-bore for nailing.

Weight: 42 lb./cu. ft.

Price: Inexpensive.

AVODIRÉ
(H)

Botanical Name: *Turreanthus africanus*
Considered to be one of the world's best quality blond woods, avodiré rarely is available in large quantities. It normally comes to North America as veneer, which possesses an attractive mottled pattern, that is used in fine cabinetmaking and paneling.
Other Names: African satinwood, African white mahogany, apeya (Ghana); apaya (Nigeria); engan (Cameroon); lusamba (Zaire); agbe (Ivory Coast); esu (Congo); African furniture wood, olon.
Sources: West and Equatorial Africa.
Characteristics: Light, strong wood; mainly straight grain but can be wavy or interlocked; medium to fine texture; golden yellow.
Uses: Cabinetwork, veneers, marquetry and plywood.
Workability: Fair; increase blade angle when planing as interlocked grain tends to cause tearout; poor bending properties; pre-bore for nailing.
Finishing: Generally good.
Weight: 36 lb./cu. ft.
Price: Expensive.

BALSA
(H)

Botanical Name: *Ochroma pyramidale*
Balsa has the lightest weight of any commercially used hardwood. This property has made it a key ingredient of life rafts and a wide variety of safety and buoyancy devices since World War II. In fact, the word balsa means raft in Spanish. Although it is difficult to dry, once it does it is a relatively stable and strong wood for its weight.
Other Names: Guano (Puerto Rico, Honduras); lanero (Cuba); polak (Belize, Nicaragua); topa (Peru); tami (Bolivia).
Sources: West Indies, Central America, tropical South America (Ecuador).
Characteristics: Straight grain; fine, velvety texture; white to oatmeal-brown with a pinkish tint.
Uses: Model-making, toys, water sports equipment and theatrical props.
Workability: Extremely good provided blades are kept very sharp; will not bend without buckling; little blunting of cutters.
Finishing: Accepts finishes well; absorbs a great quantity of finishing material.
Weight : 6-16 lb./cu. ft.
Price: Moderate.

BASSWOOD
(H)

Botanical Name: *Tilia americana*

Lightweight and easy to work, basswood has been considered one of the world's foremost carving woods for centuries. It can be shaped to remarkably fine detail. It is odor-free and has been used extensively for domestic goods such as kitchen utensils and food containers. Basswood is considered unsuitable for outdoor duty because it weathers poorly.

Other Names: American linden, linn, lime tree; American lime (U.K.).

Sources: Eastern Canada and U.S.A.

Characteristics: Straight grain; fine texture; creamy white darkening to creamy brown.

Uses: Turning, carving, pattern making, toys, piano keys, match splints, boxes and crates.

Workability: Very good; blunts cutters slightly; poor bending properties.

Finishing: Generally good with all finishes.

Weight: 26 lb./cu. ft.

Price: Inexpensive (slightly higher for thick $^{12}/_4$ and $^{16}/_4$ kiln-dried carving stock).

BAYO
(H)

Botanical Name: *Aspidosperma cruentum*

A wonderful, easy-working timber, bayo is a "lesser-known species" hardwood that is often available in large sizes and sometimes cut into veneers. Not only attractive, bayo is also very decay-resistant.

Sources: Southeast Mexico, Belize, Honduras.

Characteristics: Straight to slightly interlocking grain; medium to fine texture; heartwood: brownish pink; sapwood: cream with a pinkish blush throughout.

Uses: Cabinetwork, turning, framing, furniture and decorative veneers.

Workability: Generally good; does not take nails well; good bending properties.

Finishing: Accepts finishes well.

Weight: 37-46 lb./cu. ft.

Price: Moderate.

BEECH, AMERICAN
(H)

Botanical Name: *Fagus grandifolia*

Heavy, hard and strong, American beech is used for everything from flooring to woodenware. Although considered less attractive than European beech, American beech has prominent rays and visible tiny pores. It is highly figured when quartersawn.

Other Name: Beech.

Sources: Eastern U.S.A. and Canada.

Characteristics: Straight grain; fine, even texture; reddish brown to light brown heartwood with almost white sapwood.

Uses: Bentwood furniture, turning, handles and cabinetmaking.

Workability: Satisfactory; good with most tools but may burn when crosscut or drilled; may bind on saws; excellent turning wood; excellent bending properties; high shrinkage makes it unstable in use.

Finishing: Accepts finishes well.

Weight: 46 lb./cu. ft.

Price: Moderate.

BIRCH, PAPER
(H)

Botanical Name: *Betula papyrifera*

Paper birch is a tough, heavy wood, although it is softer than other birches. Its bark was used by Native Americans to fashion wigwams and canoes so that many people still refer to it as "canoe birch." The wood possesses an attractive figure, and is sometimes sliced into decorative veneers.

Other Names: White birch, sweet birch, American birch.

Sources: Canada, U.S.A.

Characteristics: Straight grain; fine texture; wide, creamy white sapwood; pale-brown heartwood.

Uses: Turning for domestic utensils, dowels, toothpicks, spools, bobbins, hoops and toys, plywood and decorative veneers.

Workability: Generally good; moderate dulling of cutters; unusual curly grain may pick up in planing; satisfactory bending properties.

Finishing: Accepts finishes well.

Weight: 39 lb./cu. ft.

Price: Inexpensive.

BOCOTE
(H)
Botanical Name: *Cordia spp.*
A beautiful substitute for rosewood, bocote is one of the many types of cordia—a group of hardwoods found throughout the West Indies, tropical America, Africa and Asia. Bocote's texture is similar to teak—although it is somewhat harder—and its wild figure patterns produce stunning cabinetwork. The wood is available only in small sizes.
Other Name: Cordia.
Sources: Mexico, Belize, Honduras.
Characteristics: Straight grain; moderately coarse texture; green to golden yellow with black figure patterns.
Uses: Furniture, cabinets, interior joinery, turning and decorative veneers.
Workability: Generally good; blunts cutting edges slightly; good bending properties.
Finishing: Accepts finishes well.
Weight: 48 lb./cu. ft.
Price: Expensive.

BUBINGA
(H)
Botanical name: *Guibourtia spp.*
A rosewood substitute, bubinga's logs often weigh more than 10 tons; they can be cut into extremely wide planks. Kevazingo, a veneer peeled from irregularly grained logs, possesses a wild, flame-like figure that is popular for cabinetwork.
Other Names: African rosewood, essingang, kevazingo (rotary-cut veneer only).
Sources: Equatorial Africa (Cameroon, Gabon and Zaire).
Characteristics: Very dense; fine grain; purplish pink to salmon red, with dark purple veining. Quartersawn boards often show very attractive black mottle figure.
Uses: Turning, furniture, cabinetwork and veneers.
Workability: Generally good; irregular grain tends to tear when hand-planed; pre-bore for nailing.
Finishing: Excellent.
Weight: 55 lb./cu. ft.
Price: Expensive.

BUTTERNUT
(H)

Botanical Name: *Juglans cinerea*
A member of the walnut family, butternut has assumed a place of honor as the wood often chosen for church altars. This tree is treasured for more than its wood; it possesses a rich, delicious nut and produces a sap that is used to make a sweet syrup similar to maple syrup.
Other Names: White walnut, oil nut.
Sources: Canada, U.S.A.
Characteristics: Straight grain; soft but coarse texture; medium light brown.
Uses: Furniture, interior trim on boats, interior joinery, carving, veneers.
Workability: Generally good; because wood is soft, it is important to keep cutters sharp; will fuzz up when sanded; poor bending properties.
Finishing: Accepts finishes very well.
Weight: 28 lb./cu. ft.
Price: Moderate.

CATALPA
(H)

Botanical Name: *Catalpa speciosa*
A soft, attractive wood, catalpa is a fine cabinet wood, easy to work with a wavy figure. The wood is relatively inexpensive, but often difficult to find locally. Its open grain and excessive softness make it unsuitable for furniture that will receive heavy use. Resistant to decay, it is ideal for outdoor carvings.
Other Names: Catawba, cigartree, Indian-bean, northern catalpa.
Source: U.S.A.
Characteristics: Generally uneven, wavy grain; medium coarse, even texture; light tan with a prominent darker growth ring figure.
Uses: Cabinetmaking, turning, picture frames and general ornamental uses.
Workability: Generally very good; may fray when crosscut; dulls cutters only slightly.
Finishing: Accepts finishes well.
Weight: 28-32 lb./cu. ft.
Price: Inexpensive to moderate.

CEDAR, ALASKA YELLOW
(S)

Botanical Name: *Chamaecyparis nootkatensis*

Alaska yellow cedar is stable and remarkably resistant to decay. Like most members of the cedar family, it has a distinctive odor that fades as the wood ages. This wood is not abundantly available. The trees grow to 60 to 80 feet in height in the forests of the Pacific northwest, and it can take up to 200 years for them to reach marketable size.

Other Names: Yellow cedar, Pacific Coast yellow cedar, nootka false cypress, yellow cypress.

Source: Pacific Coast of North America.

Characteristics: Straight grain; fine texture; pale yellow.

Uses: Furniture, joinery, boat building and veneers.

Workability: Very good; low dulling of cutters.

Finishing: Accepts finishes well.

Weight: 31 lb./cu. ft.

Price: Moderate.

CEDAR, AROMATIC
(S)

Botanical Name: *Juniperus virginiana*

Like most other trees known as "cedar," aromatic cedar is not botanically a "cedar" at all. In fact, the tree from which this softwood comes is a juniper. But the timber contains cedar oil and gives off the familiar "cedar" scent that is said to repel moths. These two characteristics are the reason why the wood is frequently used to line closets and chests.

Other Names: Red cedar, eastern red cedar, Tennessee red cedar, juniper.

Sources: Canada and eastern U.S.A.

Characteristics: Straight grain; fine texture; reddish-brown; boards often have knots and bark inclusions.

Uses: Carving, linings of closets and chests, veneers and pencils.

Workability: Generally good, but brittle; may break or chip when drilled; may split in nailing.

Finishing: Accepts finishes well, except for turpentine-based products.

Weight: 30 lb./cu. ft.

Price: Inexpensive.

CEDAR, WESTERN RED
(S)

Botanical Name: *Thuja plicata*

A grand-sized tree, western red cedar can grow to more than 150 feet in height. It is one of the lightest and most durable softwoods, making it ideal for outdoor use. Its distinct growth ring figure and attractive color also give it significant value for paneling and veneer. Especially knotty pieces are sold as "knotty cedar." This species is slow to regenerate; if current heavy levels of consumption do not abate, western red cedar could become a rare wood in the 21st Century.

Other Names: Giant arborvitae (U.S.A.); red cedar (Canada); British Columbia red cedar (U.K.); canoe-cedar.

Sources: Canada, U.S.A.

Characteristics: Straight grain; coarse texture.

Uses: Outdoor furniture, boat building, exterior millwork.

Workability: Generally good; keep cutters sharp.

Finishing: Accepts finishes well.

Weight: 23 lb./cu. ft.

Price: Moderate.

CEDAR, WHITE
(S)

Botanical Name: *Thuja occidentalis*

White cedar is popular in North America for its resistance to decay. It is often used for canoes, shingles and other exterior applications. While not especially strong, the wood is easy to work and is well suited to outdoor decorative objects. Smaller trees are used for poles and posts. The wood is seldom figured and almost never used as veneer.

Other Names: Arborvitae, eastern white cedar, swamp cedar.

Sources: Canada and U.S.A.

Characteristics: Straight grain; even texture; light brown heartwood; sapwood is white; many knots commonly present.

Uses: Boat building, posts and decorative fencing.

Workability: Good.

Finishing: Accepts finishes well.

Weight: 23 lb./cu. ft.

Price: Inexpensive.

CHACTACOTE
(H)

Botanical Name: *Sickingia salvadorensis*
Chactacote, a hardwood from well-managed sources, grows in the Yucatan and Chiapais regions of southeastern Mexico and Belize. Beautiful and easy to work, it is a wood of intense color and often possesses a gorgeous flame figure. It is recommended to use a finish with ultraviolet ray protectant, since its incredible hue fades with exposure to the sun.
Other Names: Chacahuante; Redwood (Belize)
Sources: Southeast Mexico, Belize.
Characteristics: Fairly irregular grain; fine texture; heartwood: brilliant crimson red; sapwood: cream.
Uses: Furniture, cabinetwork and turning.
Workability: Very good.
Finishing: Accepts finishes well.
Weight: 40-45 lb./cu. ft.
Price: Moderate.

CHERRY, BLACK
(H)

Botanical name: *Prunus serotina*
Extremely stable when it comes to checking and warping, and exceptionally beautiful, black cherry is one of North America's finest cabinet woods. However, there is a pronounced variance in color between its sapwood and heartwood, which can sometimes be problematic. If the two are used side-by-side, finished work may display a discrepancy in color, which will intensify as the wood ages. A good portion of black cherry wood contains gum deposits throughout. Although this does not significantly affect the lumber, it shows on veneers; logs with excessive gum are avoided for veneers.
Other names: American cherry, rum cherry, whiskey cherry, wild cherry, fruitwood.
Sources: Canada, U.S.A.
Characteristics: Fine grain; smooth texture; reddish brown to deep red heartwood.
Uses: Furniture, turning, carving, joinery, musical instruments, boat interiors and decorative veneers.
Workability: Very good; blunts cutting edges moderately; good bending properties.
Finishing: Accepts finishes well.
Weight: 36 lb./cu. ft.
Price: Moderate.

CHESTNUT, AMERICAN

(H)

Botanical Name: *Castanea dentata*

Virtually exterminated by a fungus disease known as chestnut blight, the majority of chestnut now comes from recycled timbers from barns and other buildings that pre-date the blight. It has also been available from standing dead trees that have been attacked by insects. The resulting "wormy chestnut" is nonetheless considered an attractive wood that retains chestnut's natural durability and makes it excellent for outdoor use.

Other Names: Wormy chestnut, sweet chestnut.

Sources: Canada and Eastern U.S.A.

Characteristics: Porous growth rings result in prominent figure; coarse texture; pale brown.

Uses: Poles, stakes, picture frames, furniture and decorative veneers.

Workability: Generally easy to work; ferrous metals may stain the wood blue; splits easily; medium bending properties.

Finishing: Accepts finishes very well.

Weight: 30 lb./cu. ft.

Price: Moderate to expensive.

CHONTAQUIRO AMARILLO

(H)

Botanical Name: *Diplotropis spp.*

A hard, heavy timber, chontaquiro amarillo is found in abundance in the tropical forests of Peru and Brazil. It is a beautiful wood, with a striking figure on both plain-sawn and quartersawn lumber. Used locally as a mahogany substitute, this lesser-known species is beginning to be exported into North America for use in fine furniture and cabinetmaking.

Other Names: Sucupira, sapupira.

Source: South America.

Characteristics: Straight to interlocked grain; moderately coarse to coarse texture; light to dark brown heartwood; yellowish cream sapwood.

Uses: Furniture, cabinetmaking and a range of construction uses.

Workability: Generally good; does not turn or shape well.

Finishing: Accepts finishes well.

Weight: 58 lb./cu. ft.

Price: Moderate.

COCOBOLO
(H)

Botanical Name: *Dalbergia retusa*
A durable, hard wood, cocobolo possesses some interesting working properties. It contains a natural oily substance that not only waterproofs the wood, but makes it very easy to work and finish. However, its fine sawdust may cause itching and sneezing and often temporarily dyes the skin orange. It is recommended to cover exposed skin when working with cocobolo.
Other Names: Granadillo (Mexico); Nicaraguan rosewood, grendill.
Source: West coast of Central America.
Characteristics: Heavy, dense wood; straight to irregular grain; medium texture; purple, orange, rust and yellow color with black markings, darkening with exposure to a deep reddish orange.
Uses: Turning, knife handles, brush backs, tool handles, inlays and veneers.
Workability: Satisfactory; significant dulling of cutters; blades should be extremely sharp; reduce blade angle for planing; very difficult to glue.
Finishing: Accepts finishes very well.
Weight: 68 lb./cu. ft.
Price: Expensive.

CYPRESS, BALD
(S)

Botanical Name: *Taxodium distichum*
Normally found in wet regions and swamps, bald cypress lumber is truly at home in water. In fact, it is often used in bridges and docks. Old-growth timber is significantly more decay-resistant than second-growth wood, though both are considered ideal for outdoor use. Mature stands of this species are becoming scarce, and as swamps are drained, it is suffering from a loss of habitat, which will make it increasingly rare as time passes. Bald cypress occasionally yields interesting veneers and paneling.
Other Names: Southern cypress, swamp cypress, tidewater cypress, yellow cypress, white cypress, red cypress, black cypress.
Source: Southeastern U.S.A.
Characteristics: Straight grain; oily texture; yellow-brown to dark brown.
Uses: Joinery, chemical vats and tanks, boat building, poles, posts and many construction applications.
Workability: Generally good; keep cutters sharp.
Finishing: Accepts finishes well.
Weight: 28-35 lb./cu. ft.
Price: Inexpensive.

DOUGLAS-FIR
(S)

Botanical Name: *Pseudotsuga menziesii*

One of the most widely used woods in North America, and the continent's most plentiful species, Douglas-fir is highly valued as a construction wood because of its strength, stiffness, moderate weight and availability of large size timbers. It is frequently spelled without the hyphen as "Douglas fir," although it is, in fact, not a fir at all but part of the genus *Pseudotsuga*, or "false hemlock." Current shortages of this lumber are due more to logging bans than any real scarcity. With its prominent growth ring figure, Douglas-fir also yields attractive veneers and plywood.

Other Names: British Columbia pine, Oregon pine, yellow fir, red fir.

Sources: Canada, Western U.S.A., Europe.

Characteristics: Straight grain; medium texture; reddish brown; may be resinous.

Uses: Plywood, joinery, veneers and a wide range of construction applications.

Workability: Generally good; better with machine tools; blunts cutters moderately.

Finishing: Accepts finishes fairly well.

Weight: 33 lb./cu. ft.

Price: Inexpensive.

EBONY
(H)

Botanical Name: *Diospyros spp.*

All ebony is rare and expensive, especially the famed, intense black ebony which, at one time, was obtained primarily from India and Sri Lanka. Today, it is found in limited quantities in areas of Equatorial West Africa. Unlike Macassar ebony, African ebony is generally solid black, without stripes or mottling. Shipped to North America in short heartwood billets, it is used in the finest wood objects. Sawdust from ebony can cause respiratory problems.

Other Names: Batulinau, Indian ebony, Ceylon ebony, African ebony, Madagascar ebony, Gabon ebony etc., according to country of origin.

Sources: India, Sri Lanka, Africa.

Characteristics: Dense wood with a coarse texture; straight to interlocked grain; very dark brown to black.

Uses: Turnings, brush backs, musical instruments, handles, inlay, butts of billiard cues, occasionally veneers and other highly decorative applications.

Workability: Difficult; dulls cutters severely; pre-bore for nailing.

Finishing: Accepts finishes well.

Weight: 65 lb./cu. ft.

Price: Very expensive.

EBONY, MACASSAR
(H)

Botanical Name: *Diospyros spp.*
Macassar ebony, unlike black ebony with its intense deep hue, is multicolored, usually more light than dark. Both Macassar ebony and black ebony are used in the finest inlay and cabinet work. Macassar ebony comes from a number of different species that are all part of the ebony family; there may be some variation in density, texture and appearance from one piece to another.
Other Names: Calamander wood, coromandel (U.K.); golden ebony, marblewood.
Source: Southeast Asia.
Characteristics: Extremely dense with very brittle heartwood; mostly straight grain, but may be irregular or wavy; fine, even texture; dark brown to black, with light-brown streaks.
Uses: Cabinetwork, turnings, brush backs, walking sticks, musical instruments, inlay work, billiard cues and decorative veneers; sapwood used for tool handles.
Workability: Very difficult; extreme blunting of cutters; pre-bore for nailing; unsuitable for gluing.
Finishing: Accepts finishes very well.
Weight: 60-80 lb./cu. ft.
Price: Very expensive.

ELM, WHITE
(H)

Botanical Name: *Ulmus americana*
White elm is the largest and arguably the most stately elm of all. More so than other elms, this majestic tree was devastated by Dutch elm disease and today it is relatively difficult to find white elm lumber. The wood is extremely easy to bend and is most often used to make furniture. When sliced on the quarter, white elm produces lovely ribbon-striped veneers.
Other Names: American elm, water elm, swamp elm (U.S.A.); orhamwood, gray elm (Canada).
Sources: Canada and U.S.A.
Characteristics: Usually straight grain, though often interlocked; coarse texture; light, yellowish-brown color.
Uses: Furniture, boat building, sports equipment and decorative veneers.
Workability: Generally good; dulls cutting edges moderately; good bending properties, but prone to warping.
Finishing: Accepts finishes well.
Weight: 35 lb./cu. ft.
Price: Inexpensive, but increasing due to scarcity.

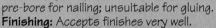

GONCALO ALVES

(H)
Botanical name: *Astronium graveolens*
Beautiful, durable and strong, goncalo alves sometimes bears a resemblance to both rosewood and Macassar ebony. It is used for fine applications like knife handles, billiard cue butts, brush backs, and dampers in grand pianos. Because the tree has become an endangered species, goncalo alves is difficult to find in North America. It is available primarily in veneers.
Other Name: Tigerwood
Source: Brazil.
Characteristics: Dense, very heavy wood; irregular, interlocked grain; medium texture; reddish-brown marbled with black streaks; large variations in color and grain.
Uses: Fine furniture, cabinetmaking, turning and veneers.
Workability: Difficult; blunts cutting edges moderately to severely; pre-bore for nailing.
Finishing: Accepts finishes well.
Weight: 59 lb./cu. ft.
Price: Expensive.

HACKBERRY

(H)
Botanical Name: *Celtis occidentalis*
Hackberry is elastic, shock-resistant and easy to bend, characteristics it shares with elm and ash; it is often used as an ash substitute in the furniture industry. Hackberry trees grow to more than 100 feet tall. Although most hackberry is used for construction, the wood's distinct figure makes it an attractive choice for veneers, cabinetwork and furniture.
Other Names: Sugarberry, hack-tree, bastard elm, nettletree, beaverwood.
Sources: Eastern U.S.A. and southern Canada.
Characteristics: Irregular grain; moderately coarse texture; light brown with yellow bands.
Uses: Furniture, sports equipment, cabinetwork, plywood and veneers.
Workability: Generally good; dulls cutters moderately; interlocked grain requires reduced planing angle; good bending properties.
Finishing: Accepts finishes well; especially attractive in natural color.
Weight: 40 lb./cu. ft.
Price: Inexpensive.

HICKORY
(H)

Botanical Name: *Carya spp.*

For strength, hardness and flexibility, hickory is the best commercially available wood in North America. It is used for tool handles, such as axes and mauls, and for sporting equipment. Even its wood chips are useful; they are often used in smoking meat.

Other Names: Shagbark hickory, pignut hickory, mockernut hickory, red hickory, white hickory.

Source: Eastern U.S.A.

Characteristics: Normally straight grain, but can be irregular or wavy; coarse texture; brown to reddish-brown heartwood; white sapwood.

Uses: Sporting equipment, bentwood furniture, chairs, striking handles, plywood and veneers.

Workability: Difficult; blunts cutting edges moderately; when planing irregular grain, reduce blade's cutting angle; very good bending properties.

Finishing: Accepts finishes well.

Weight: 51 lb./cu. ft.

Price: Inexpensive.

HOLLY
(H)

Botanical Name: *Ilex spp.*

A close-grained, almost white wood, with virtually no visible figure, holly is valued for inlay work. Holly veneer, dyed black, substitutes for ebony. Very little of this timber is cut each year, making it a difficult wood to obtain. Sprigs of holly, however, with their shiny leaves and red berries, are common Christmas decorations.

Other Names: White holly.

Sources: Europe, U.S.A. and western Asia.

Characteristics: Irregular grain; fine, even texture; white to grayish-white; prone to blue stain.

Uses: Ornate turnings, musical instruments, inlay, marquetry and veneers.

Workability: Difficult; keep cutting edges very sharp and reduce cutting angle of plane blade.

Finishing: Accepts finishes very well.

Weight: 35-50 lb./cu. ft.

Price: Expensive.

IMBUIA

(H)

Botanical Name: *Phoebe porosa*

Imbuia is a rich wood, sometimes beautifully figured, and most commonly seen in North America in veneer and paneling. The wood has a peculiar, but not unpleasant, spicy odor and taste. Its sawdust may cause irritation and sneezing for some people.

Other Names: Amarela, Brazilian walnut, canella, embuia, imbuya.

Source: Brazil.

Characteristics: Usually straight, but frequently wavy grain; fine texture; olive or yellow to chocolate brown with visible growth rings.

Uses: Fine furniture and cabinetmaking, joinery, gunstocks, paneling and veneers.

Workability: Generally good; dulls cutters slightly; poor bending properties.

Finishing: Accepts finishes very well.

Weight: 41 lb./cu. ft.

Price: Moderate.

IROKO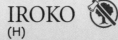

(H)

Botanical Name: *Chlorophora excelsa*

Sometimes marketed as African teak, iroko compares favorably with that wood in its strength, durability and stability. In appearance, it is rather less stunning, though its broken stripe veneers are attractive for cabinetwork. Not especially popular in North America, iroko logs are sometimes marred by deposits commonly called "stone," which makes them difficult to work. The wood's sawdust can cause respiratory problems.

Other Names: African teak, framere, intule, ireme, kambala, moreira, mvulu, Nigerian teak, odoum, oroko, tule.

Source: Equatorial Africa.

Characteristics: Interlocked or irregular grain; coarse, even texture; light golden to dark brown.

Use: Boat building, joinery, cabinetwork, furniture (particularly outdoor), carving, plywood and veneers.

Workability: Generally good; stone deposits may dull cutters moderately to severely; medium bending properties; reduce blade cutting angle when planing.

Finishing: Accepts finishes very well when filled.

Weight: 40 lb./cu. ft.

Price: Moderate.

JATOBA
(H)

Botanical Name: *Hymenaea courbaril*
A strong, hard wood, jatoba has shock-resistance qualities similar to ash and hickory, and is often used in tool handles and sports equipment. Although a difficult wood to work, jatoba takes on a special glow when it is planed. Its bark is similar to that of paper birch and sheets of it are used in canoe-making.
Other Names: Amerelo, cuapinol, courbaril, West Indian locust (U.S.A., U.K.); locust, stinking toe (West Indies); guapinol (Central America); jutaby, jatai vermelho (Brazil); algarrobo.
Sources: Central and South America and the West Indies.
Characteristics: Mostly interlocked grain; medium to coarse texture; salmon red to orange brown heartwood with dark brown streaks, darkening to reddish brown; white to pinkish sapwood.
Uses: Furniture, cabinetmaking, turning, tool handles, sporting equipment, flooring, paneling and veneers.
Workability: Fair; tough to saw; interlocked grain hard to plane; poor for nailing; moderate bending properties.
Finishing: Accepts stains well, but does not polish to a high-gloss finish.
Weight: 48-56 lb./cu. ft.
Price: Moderate.

KINGWOOD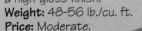
(H)

Botanical Name: *Dalbergia cearensis*
Like most rosewoods, kingwood is heavy and very attractive. Deserving of its regal name, this timber was used in the finest furniture built for Louis XIV and Louis XV of France. Today, kingwood is an endangered species that is becoming extremely scarce. The small amounts that are available find use in restoration work, fine turnings and veneers.
Other Names: Violetwood, violetta (U.S.A.); violete (Brazil).
Source: Brazil.
Characteristics: Straight grain; fine texture; violet-brown, dark violet and black stripes against yellow to violet-brown background.
Uses: Turning and veneers for inlay and marquetry.
Workability: Generally good; blunts tool and blade cutting edges moderately.
Finishing: Accepts finishes well; well suited to a natural wax finish.
Weight: 70-75 lb./cu. ft.
Price: Very expensive.

KOA
(H)

Botanical Name: *Acacia koa*

Hawaii's principal timber, koa has for centuries been used for a wide range of construction and woodworking applications. It grows almost anywhere on the islands, from sea level to mountain top. Perhaps most famous for its use in ukuleles and guitars, the wood is becoming increasingly scarce due to its limited natural range. Its use in continental North America is primarily as a veneer, which often features a stunning fiddleback figure.

Other Name: Hawaiian mahogany.

Source: Hawaiian Islands.

Characteristics: Interlocked, often curly or wavy grain; medium texture; reddish to dark brown with dark lines and markings.

Uses: High-grade furniture and cabinetwork, musical instruments, interior joinery, gunstocks and veneers.

Workability: Generally good; blunts cutters moderately; reduce blade cutting angle when shaping or planing curly grain; medium bending properties.

Finishing: Accepts finishes very well.

Weight: 41 lb./cu. ft.

Price: Expensive.

LACEWOOD
(H)

Botanical Names: *Cardwellia sublimis; Grevillea robusta*

The two botanical names given here denote two related, but separate, species; the name lacewood is usually used for Cardwellia, while Grevillea is more often called silky-oak. Both trees are large and offer similar timbers, resembling light mahogany in color, though lacewood has a much more striking quartersawn figure. The sawdust may cause a rash or respiratory problems for some people.

Other Names: Silky-oak, selena, louro faia.

Sources: Australia, Brazil.

Characteristics: Usually straight grain with large rays; moderately coarse texture; reddish-brown.

Uses: Furniture, turning, joinery, plywood and veneers.

Workability: Generally good; reduce cutting angle for planing; rays on quartersawn pieces tend to separate easily from surrounding tissue during milling or sanding; good bending properties.

Finishing: Accepts finishes well.

Weight: 34 lb./cu. ft.

Price: Moderate.

LIGNUM VITAE

(H)

Botanical Name: *Guaiacum officinale*

Lignum vitae or "wood of life" received its name for the supposedly curative qualities of its resin. This species, which is extremely slow-growing, produces one of the world's heaviest commercial timbers, and is virtually self-lubricating due to its high resin content. This makes it ideal for its principal use, as bearings and bushing blocks for ship propellor shafts, for which there is presently no effective synthetic substitute.

Other Names: Ironwood (U.S.A.); guayacan negro, palo santo (Cuba); bois de gaiac (France).

Sources: Tropical America and West Indies.

Characteristics: Heavy, dense wood; interlocked, irregular grain; greenish-brown to black.

Uses: Marine bearings, mallet heads, pulleys and turnings.

Workability: Difficult; dulls cutters moderately; not suitable for gluing unless treated first.

Finishing: Accepts finishes well.

Weight: 77 lb./cu. ft.

Price: Very expensive.

MADRONE

(H)

Botanical Name: *Arbutus menziesii*

Madrone varies greatly in size, some trees reaching 125 feet in height with enormous branches sometimes stretching out over an area of 10,000 square feet. It offers a beautiful timber, which, though difficult to dry, can be given a remarkably smooth finish. Smaller madrone timber often has burl growths at its base; these are frequently developed into stunning veneers. It is also known as one of the best sources of charcoal for making gunpowder.

Other Names: Pacific madrone, arbutus, madrona.

Sources: Canada and western U.S.A.

Characteristics: Straight to irregular grain; fine, even texture; pale reddish-yellow to deeper red or brown.

Uses: Fine furniture, turning and decorative veneers.

Workability: Satisfactory; blunts cutting edges rather severely; medium bending properties.

Finishing: Accepts finishes well.

Weight: 48 lb./cu. ft.

Price: Moderate.

MAHOGANY, AFRICAN
(H)

Botanical Name: *Khaya spp.*

Occurring over a vast region of that continent, African mahogany is an immense tree, capable of growing to 200 feet in height. The wood, available in a wide range of sizes, is slightly more difficult to work than its South American cousin, but the reward, in its fine appearance and stunning figures, is great.

Other Names: Khaya; Nigerian, Benin, Lagos, Ghana and Ivory Coast mahogany.

Sources: West, Central and East Africa.

Characteristics: Straight to interlocked grain; moderately coarse texture; reddish-brown.

Uses: Cabinetmaking, joinery, furniture, boat building, plywood and veneers.

Workability: Fair; dulls cutting edges moderately; may tear, pick up, or become woolly in cutting and planing; poor bending properties.

Finishing: Accepts finishes very well.

Weight: 34-36 lb./cu. ft.

Price: Moderate.

MAHOGANY, SOUTH AMERICAN
(H)

Botanical Name: *Swietenia macrophylla*

Not only one of the most valuable timbers in South and Central America, this species is also, without a doubt, one of the foremost cabinet woods in the world. While it is sometimes used in ship and boat building because of its combination of stability, durability and light weight, its primary use is in the finest furniture and reproduction work.

Other Names: Caoba, acajou; Central American, Honduras, Peruvian, Brazilian, Costa Rican, Nicaraguan mahogany etc., according to the country of origin.

Sources: Central and South America.

Characteristics: Straight to interlocked grain; medium coarse texture; light reddish-brown to medium red.

Uses: Fine furniture, interior paneling, moldings and joinery, boat interiors, pianos, carving, pattern making, and a wide range of decorative veneers.

Workability: Generally good; blades must be kept sharp; moderate bending properties.

Finishing: Excellent with all finishes.

Weight: 34-40 lb./cu. ft.

Price: Moderate.

MAPLE, HARD
(H)

Botanical Name: *Acer saccharum*

A dense wood, hard maple's uses often take advantage of its resistance to wear and abrasion. It is used in a wide range of construction, including bowling alleys and dance floors. Often possessing an attractive fiddleback or curly figure, this is also the maple which produces the famous bird's-eye veneers.

Other Names: Rock maple, sugar maple, white maple (sapwood), bird's-eye maple (if the distinguishing grain is present).

Sources: Canada, U.S.A.

Characteristics: Straight grain, occasionally curly, wavy or bird's-eye; fine texture; heartwood is reddish brown; sapwood is white.

Uses: Turning, furniture, sports equipment, musical instruments, butcher's blocks, flooring, plywood and veneers.

Workability: Difficult; blunts cutting edges moderately; pre-bore for nailing; good bending properties.

Finishing: Accepts finishes well.

Weight: 42 lb./cu. ft.

Price: Inexpensive to moderate, depending on figure.

MYRTLE
(H)

Botanical Name: *Umbellularia californica*

Especially well known for its cluster and burl figured veneers, myrtle is a favorite among fine craftsmen for cabinetmaking and marquetry. While it has a strong tendency to check and warp in drying, once seasoned myrtle is a tough wood, able to withstand much wear and abuse. Also a preferred turning wood, myrtle is frequently made into bowls and candlesticks, among other fine goods.

Other Names: California laurel, mountain laurel, baytree, spicetree.

Sources: Oregon and California, U.S.A.

Characteristics: Generally straight grain, but occasionally irregular; fine texture; golden tan to yellowish-green.

Uses: Turning, furniture, joinery, cabinetmaking, paneling, and veneers.

Workability: Fair; dulls cutting edges severely and quickly; reduce cutting angle for planing and shaping.

Finishing: Accepts finishes very well.

Weight: 38 lb./cu. ft.

Price: Moderate; burl is expensive.

OAK, RED
(H)

Botanical name: *Quercus spp.*

Red oak, the most common oak variety in North America, grows very quickly—young trees often sprout a foot a year. The wood is an attractive and valuable hardwood and has been one of the most popular North American oaks used in Europe since the early 18th Century. It is considered unsuitable for exterior work.

Other Names: Northern red oak, American red oak, Canadian red oak, gray oak.

Sources: Canada and eastern U.S.A.

Characteristics: Straight grain; coarse texture; pinkish-red color.

Uses: Furniture, interior joinery, flooring, plywood and veneers.

Workability: Generally good; moderate blunting of cutters; moderate bending properties.

Finishing: Satisfactory; because of open pores, it should be filled before any finishing or painting.

Weight: 40 lb./cu. ft.

Price: Moderate.

OAK, WHITE
(H)

Botanical Name: *Quercus spp.*

This oak—a wood of unique versatility—produces the finest oak veneers and lumber, and is very resistant to wear. These qualities make it significantly more valuable than red oak. But perhaps its most-valued property is the presence in its cells of tyloses, a honeycomblike substance that makes the wood watertight and ideal for whiskey barrels. Recently, these barrels have begun to be reused, reducing the large drain on white oak for that purpose.

Other Names: American white oak, burr oak, swamp white oak, chestnut oak, overcup oak, swamp chestnut oak.

Sources: Canada and U.S.A.

Characteristics: Straight grain; moderately coarse texture; light tan with a yellowish tint.

Uses: Furniture, joinery, cabinetmaking, boat building, barrels, plywood and veneers.

Workability: Good; pre-bore for nailing; good bending properties.

Finishing: Accepts finishes well.

Weight: 47 lb./cu. ft.

Price: Moderate.

OLIVEWOOD
(H)

Botanical Name: *Olea europaea*

Grown along the Mediterranean coast, European olivewood is a comely tree, and yields a fine, attractive wood that emits a sweet scent when it is worked. This tree is also famous for its fruit and oil. Available in very small amounts, and prone to defects, olivewood is often used to produce small turned or carved goods for sale in Europe's tourist market, and it is sometimes cut into veneer.

Other Name: Italian olivewood.

Sources: Italy and southern Europe, California.

Characteristics: Straight to irregular grain; fine texture; light to dark brown background with darker streaks.

Uses: Turning, carving and inlay work.

Workability: Generally good, though relatively difficult to saw.

Finishing: Accepts finishes well.

Weight: 58 lb./cu. ft.

Price: Expensive

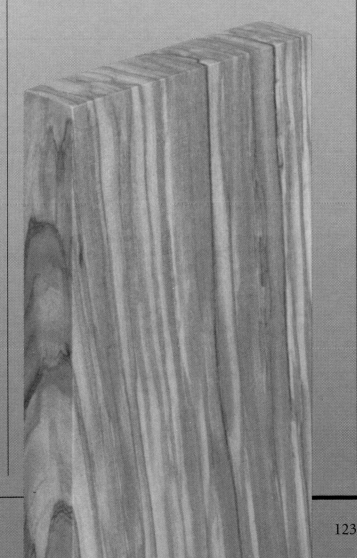

PADAUK, AFRICAN
(H)

Botanical Name: *Pterocarpus soyauxii*

African padauk is extremely strong, durable and stable. Though less well-known than the rare Andaman padauk, it compares well, is much more available and is truly a handsome wood in its own right. In some parts of the world African padauk is commonly used for flooring, where it is considered of exceptional quality; padauk veneers are no less valued for their beauty.

Other Names: Padouk, barwood, camwood.

Source: West Africa.

Characteristics: Straight to interlocked grain; moderately coarse texture; deep red to purple-brown with red streaks.

Uses: Furniture, cabinetmaking, joinery, turning, handles and veneers.

Workability: Good; dulls cutters slightly.

Finishing: Accepts finishes very well.

Weight: 45 lb./cu. ft.

Price: Moderate.

PAU FERRO
(H)

Botanical Name: *Machaerium spp.*

Sometimes referred to by the generic term "iron-wood," pau ferro has no significant history of use in North America, despite its similarity to the rose-woods. However, with the current extremely limited supply of Brazilian rosewood, pau ferro has assumed a position of greater prominence, particularly for woodworkers. As the rosewoods become scarce, its use will no doubt increase.

Other Names: Caviuna, moradillo, santos rosewood; capote, siete cueros (Colombia); cascaron (Venezuela); chiche (Ecuador); tuseque, morado (Bolivia); jacaranda, jacaranda pardo (Brazil).

Source: South America (primarily Bolivia and Brazil).

Characteristics: Straight to irregular grain; fine to coarse texture; heartwood, light to medium brown or purple with dark growth lines; grayish sapwood.

Uses: Turning, musical instruments, fine furniture, cabinetwork and veneers.

Workability: Ranges from fair to good. The dust may cause skin and respiratory problems.

Finishing: Accepts finishes well.

Weight: 49-60 lb./cu. ft.

Price: Expensive.

PEAR
(H)

Botanical name: *Pyrus communis*

Pearwood is a relatively rare lumber, available in small sizes for highly specialized uses. The tree itself grows to a height of only about 50 feet and is primarily valued for its fruit. In fact, much available pearwood comes from old orchard trees. Because of its fine workability, it is ideal for carving.

Other Name: Swiss pear.

Sources: Europe, U.S.A. and western Asia.

Characteristics: Straight grain; very fine, even texture; pinkish-brown.

Uses: Carving, turning, brush backs, recorders, piano keys and decorative veneers.

Workability: Medium; moderate blunting of cutters; excellent turning wood.

Finishing: Excellent, particularly for staining; often dyed black to resemble ebony in veneer form.

Weight: 44 lb./cu. ft.

Price: Expensive.

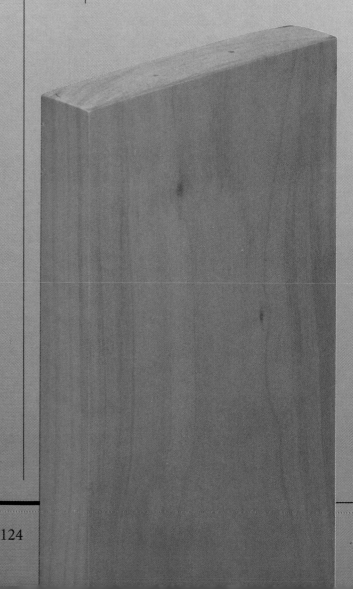

PECAN
(H)

Botanical Name: *Carya spp.* (primarily *Carya illinoensis*)
A member of the hickory genus, what is known as pecan actually comes from several species of trees whose wood is often marketed with—or even as—true hickory. The two are distinguishable, however, by the deep red color markings or streaks in pecan's heartwood and by weight. True hickory is slightly heavier. Though often undervalued, pecan is a fine, attractive wood, its veneers often containing a beautiful mottled figure. And of course, like hickory, it has exceptional qualities of strength.
Other Names: Pecan hickory, sweet pecan, water hickory, bitter pecan, bitternut hickory.
Sources: Mexico and U.S.A.
Characteristics: Straight-grained though sometimes irregular or wavy; coarse texture; heartwood is reddish brown; sapwood is white.
Uses: Turning, furniture, tool handles, sports equipment, drumsticks and veneers.
Workability: Fair; can dull cutting edges severely; reduce cutting angle when planing or shaping irregular grain; pre-bore for nailing; very good bending properties.
Finishing: Accepts finishes well.
Weight: 46 lb./cu. ft.
Price: Moderate.

PERSIMMON
(H)

Botanical Name: *Diospyros virginiana*
Although it belongs to the same genus as the famous black ebony, the nearly white sapwood of the persimmon is most valued. Persimmon's dark wood is limited to its small heartwood core and is rarely of interest to the woodworker. Known for its shock resistance, hardness and finishing qualities, persimmon is used for golf club heads. Occasionally, logs are sliced into veneers which can have an attractive figure.
Other Names: Boa wood, bara-bara, butter wood, cylil date plum, virginia date plum, possum wood, American ebony.
Sources: Central and southern U.S.A.
Characteristics: Straight grain; fine, even texture; may have dark brown or black streaks; sapwood is off-white.
Uses: Golf club heads, turning and veneers; sometimes flooring and furniture.
Workability: Generally good; dulls cutting edges moderately; reduce cutting angle when planing; pre-bore for nailing; moderate bending properties; high shrinkage makes it unstable in use.
Finishing: Accepts finishes very well.
Weight: 52 lb./cu. ft.
Price: Inexpensive to moderate.

PINE, PONDEROSA
(S)

Botanical Name: *Pinus ponderosa*

One of the most attractive pines, the ponderosa grows across western North America and sometimes makes its home at elevations of more than 10,000 feet in the Rockies. Because of its resemblance in color and texture to white pine, ponderosa has increasingly been used as a substitute for that wood. Ponderosa pine is sometimes sliced into knotty pine veneer, but its primary use is in construction and as interior trim.

Other Names: Big pine, bird's-eye pine, knotty pine, pole pine, prickly pine, western yellow pine.

Sources: Canada and western U.S.A.

Characteristics: Wide light-yellow sapwood; darker yellow to reddish-brown heartwood; generally straight grain; even texture.

Uses: Furniture, turning and carving (sapwood); joinery and general construction (heartwood); occasionally paneling and veneers.

Workability: Good; blunts cutting edges slightly; poor bending properties.

Finishing: Accepts finishes well, but does not stain as well as white pine.

Weight: 32 lb./cu. ft.

Price: Inexpensive.

PINE, SOUTHERN YELLOW
(S)

Botanical Name: *Pinus spp.*

Southern yellow pine is the heaviest commercial softwood and certainly of foremost importance for the construction and pulp industries. But, because of the decreasing supply of white pine, it has recently begun to be used extensively in veneers, which are darker and marked by distinct growth rings. These trees also supply turpentine, pine oil and resin used in the cosmetics industry.

Other Names: Pitch pine, short leaf pine, long leaf pine, loblolly pine and several other tree names.

Source: Southeastern U.S.A.

Characteristics: Straight grain; coarse texture; yellow-brown to reddish-brown heartwood.

Uses: Furniture, construction, plywood and veneers.

Workability: Fair; high resin content will cause gummy build-up on tools; tends to tear when crosscut.

Finishing: Accepts finishes fairly well; because of high resin content, finishes sometimes bubble up, especially around knots.

Weight: 30-38 lb./cu. ft.

Price: Inexpensive.

PINE, WHITE
(S)

Botanical Name: *Pinus strobus*

White pine's versatility, workability and non-resinous nature made it a preferred wood for both construction and woodworking for centuries. Early American settlers often honored the white pine, putting it on the colonies' flag during the American Revolution and on other flags and coins through the years. Unfortunately, because of its widespread use, white pine has become scarcer, although second generation stands are presently maturing.

Other Names: Eastern white pine, northern white pine, northern pine, Quebec pine, soft pine, balsam pine, Canadian white pine.

Sources: Canada and U.S.A.

Characteristics: Straight grain; even texture; light-yellow to reddish-brown heartwood.

Uses: Furniture, joinery, boat building, construction, plywood and veneers.

Workability: Good; blunts cutters slightly; poor bending properties; too soft for some furniture uses.

Finishing: Accepts finishes well.

Weight: 28 lb./cu. ft.

Price: Inexpensive.

POPLAR, YELLOW
(H)

Botanical Names: *Liriodendron tulipifera*

Much of the remaining supply of this wood, regarded as one of the most valuable timbers in the eastern U.S.A., lies in the Appalachian Mountains. Used extensively in Europe in the early 1900s, today the wood is used mainly in the U.S. for a range of woodworking applications and for pulp. The sapwood is sometimes called whitewood.

Other Names: Canoe wood, tulip poplar, tuliptree.

Source: U.S.A.

Characteristics: Straight grain; fine, even texture; white sapwood to pale-brown heartwood with green or dark brown streaks.

Uses: Joinery, furniture, cabinetwork, musical instruments, carving and veneers.

Workability: Good; dulls cutters only slightly.

Finishing: Accepts finishes well.

Weight: 30-35 lb./cu. ft.

Price: Inexpensive.

PRIMAVERA
(H)

Botanical Names: *Cybistax donnell-smithii,*
syn. Tabebuia donnell-smithii

Sometimes wrongly referred to as "white mahogany,"
primavera is one of the finest "blond" cabinet woods in
the world. Because of the depletion of supply, however,
today it is relatively hard to get. The wood is well known
for its beautiful light-colored veneers. Often they are
striped or have a handsome mottled figure.

Other Names: Duranga (Mexico); San Juan (Honduras);
palo blanco (Guatemala); cortez, cortez blanco
(El Salvador).

Source: Central America.

Characteristics: Straight to irregular grain; medium to
coarse texture; yellowish-white to yellowish-brown.

Uses: Cabinet work, fine furniture and veneers.

Workability: Very good; moderate bending properties.

Finishing: Accepts finishes very well.

Weight: 30-38 lb./cu. ft.

Price: Expensive.

PURPLEHEART
(H)

Botanical Name: *Peltogyne spp.*

A uniquely attractive and durable hardwood and a challenge to work with. Cutting can be hampered by gum
deposits, which will seep out of the wood if it is heated
with blunt cutting edges. Blades, therefore, must be
kept extremely sharp, and wood should be run slowly
through machines. While the wood is purple, these gum
deposits can range from coal black to white, and often
streak the wood.

Other Names: Amaranth, violetwood (U.S.A.); sakavalli,
saka, koroboreli (Guyana); pau roxo, nazareno (Venezuela);
pau roxo, amarante (Brazil); tananeo (Colombia).

Sources: Central and South America.

Characteristics: Straight grain; moderate to coarse
texture; deep purple, maturing to a rich brown after
long exposure.

Uses: Veneers, turning, indoor and outdoor, furniture,
tool shafts and handles, and butts of billiard cues.

Workability: Difficult; moderate to severe blunting; pre-
bore for nailing; moderate bending properties.

Finishing: Accepts finishes well; lacquer preserves purple color; alcohol-based finishes remove the color.

Weight: 54 lb./cu. ft.

Price: Moderate.

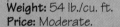

REDWOOD, CALIFORNIA
(S)

Botanical Name: *Sequoia sempervirens*
The fascinating California redwood grows to an incredible size. Native to coastal California and Oregon, it is capable of reaching well over 300 feet in height and one tree may yield thousands of board feet of lumber. Although supplies of this wood have been seriously depleted, redwood can sometimes still be acquired in extremely wide planks. The wood is noted for its stability, durability and resistance to decay; its large burls are cut into veneers.
Other Name: Redwood.
Source: West coast of U.S.A.
Characteristics: Straight grain; fine, even texture; deep reddish-brown.
Uses: Joinery, furniture, posts, paneling, plywood and veneers, and much light outdoor construction.
Workability: Good; dulls cutters only slightly; moderate bending properties.
Finishing: Accepts finishes well.
Weight: 26 lb./cu. ft.
Price: Inexpensive to moderate.

ROSEWOOD, HONDURAS
(H)

Botanical Name: *Dalbergia stevensonii*
This hard, heavy, durable rosewood is primarily valued in the making of marimba bars and grows only in Belize, the former British Honduras. As supplies are very limited, its other main uses are confined to fine cabinetwork, marquetry and turned items. Some specimens are very oily and will not take a high natural polish.
Other Name: Nagaed.
Source: Belize.
Characteristics: Straight to somewhat streaked grain; moderately fine texture; pinkish-brown to purple with dark, irregular grain lines.
Uses: Musical instruments, veneers for fine cabinetwork and turning.
Workability: Fair; tough to machine because of hardness; severely dulls cutting edges; poor bending properties.
Finishing: Accepts finishes well, provided the wood is not too oily.
Weight : 60 lb./cu. ft.
Price: Expensive.

ROSEWOOD, INDONESIAN

(H)

Botanical Name: *Dalbergia latifolia*

Originating in India, this fine wood is the same species as Indian rosewood and is one of the most important timbers in both of its native lands. Incredibly stable, it is especially valued for the most precise cabinetwork. In North America, it is used both in solid form and as veneer. Because of the tree's large size, the veneer can be cut on the true quarter, producing a striped effect.

Other Names: Shisham, biti, eravidi, kalaruk (India); East Indian rosewood, Bombay rosewood.

Sources: Java and Southern India.

Characteristics: Interlocked grain; medium coarse, even texture; golden brown to dark purple-brown with almost black streaks.

Uses: Fine furniture, cabinetmaking, musical instruments, turning, joinery and veneers.

Workability: Difficult; dulls cutting edges severely; good bending properties; not suited to nailing.

Finishing: Accepts finishes very well.

Weight: 53 lb./cu. ft.

Price: Expensive.

SAPELE

(S)

Botanical Name: *Entandrophragma cylindricum*

A tree of considerable size, sapele produces logs as great as five feet in diameter. It also yields a range of remarkable figured veneers. This wood is heavier, harder, stronger and usually more prominently figured than African mahogany, for which it is sometimes mistaken. It is often available quartersawn.

Other Names: Aboudikro (Ivory Coast); penkwa (Ghana); muyovu (Uganda); sapelli (Cameroon); libuyu (Zaire); sapelewood (Nigeria); acajou sapele.

Sources: East and West Africa.

Characteristics: Interlocked grain; moderately fine texture; heartwood medium to dark reddish-brown; sapwood light yellow; cedar scent.

Uses: Cabinetwork, joinery, furniture, plywood, boat building, musical instruments, sports equipment, paneling, marquetry and veneers.

Workability: Satisfactory; will sometimes tear on interlocked grain in planing; moderate bending properties.

Finishing: Accepts finishes well.

Weight: 42 lb./cu. ft.

Price: Moderate.

SASSAFRAS
(H)

Botanical Name: *Sassafras albidum*

Sassafras, a member of the same family as cinnamon, is best known for its fragrant oil, used for flavoring and scenting, and the tea made from its root bark. While similar in color, grain and texture to black ash, sassafras timber is brittle and soft and is seldom available in large sizes. Its decay resistance and resonance make it an attractive choice for some specialized applications.

Other Names: Cinnamon wood, red sassafras, gumbo file.

Source: Eastern U.S.A.

Characteristics: Straight grain; coarse texture; light to dark brown.

Uses: Boat building, kayak paddles, containers, furniture and musical instruments.

Workability: Fair; wood is brittle and soft, so keep tool edges very sharp; pre-bore for nailing to avoid splitting; good bending properties.

Finishing: Accepts finishes well.

Weight: 28 lb./cu. ft.

Price: Inexpensive to moderate.

SATINWOOD, CEYLON
(H)

Botanical Name: *Chloroxylon swietenia*

Though the name satinwood has been given to many world timbers, Ceylon satinwood is one of very few that have found significant use in North America. It has been used in fine woodworking and cabinetmaking for centuries, but today is valued mainly for its stunning veneers—especially the famous bee's-wing mottle. In solid form it generally is used for fine turned goods such as brush backs, recorders and inlay work.

Other Names: East Indian satinwood, yellow sanders; billu, mashwal (India); Ceylon satinwood (Sri Lanka).

Sources: India and Sri Lanka.

Characteristics: Interlocked grain; fine, even texture; light yellow to gold.

Uses: Cabinetmaking, furniture, turning, joinery and decorative veneers.

Workability: Difficult; grain tends to tear in planing quartersawn material; good bending properties.

Finishing: Accepts finishes well when filled.

Weight: 61 lb./cu. ft.

Price: Expensive.

SNAKEWOOD
(H)

Botanical Names: *Piratinera guianensis*,
syn. *Brosimum guianensis*

Its markings, which resemble those on snakeskin, give this small, relatively rare timber its name. Found in limited quantities in Guyana and Surinam, it is predominantly used in turned items and carries a certain cachet . A snakewood cane or umbrella, for instance, might be considered a precious possession. Because of its hardness, snakewood is very difficult to work.

Other Names: Letterwood, leopardwood, speckled wood.
Source: South America.
Characteristics: Straight grain; fine, even texture; deep red to reddish-brown with irregular, horizontal black markings.
Uses: Fine turned goods, violin bows, knife handles, marquetry and veneers.
Workability: Difficult; dulls cutting edges.
Finishing: Accepts finishes well.
Weight: 81 lb./cu. ft.
Price: Very expensive.

SPANISH CEDAR
(H)

Botanical Name: *Cedrela spp.*

Although many species are marketed under the name Spanish cedar, the most important in the North American wood trade, Cedrela mexicana, grows in Central America and Mexico. Extremely prized in its native region for its stability, weathering qualities and relative strength, it is exported on a very limited scale. Like other "cedars," this hardwood will arouse the senses with a pleasant aroma.

Other Names: Brazilian cedar, Honduras cedar, cedro, cedro rouge.
Sources: Mexico, Central and South America.
Characteristics: Straight, occasionally interlocked, grain: fine to coarse, uneven texture; pinkish-to reddish-brown heartwood, darkens with exposure to a deeper red, occasionally with a purple tint; sapwood is white to pink.
Uses: Furniture, cabinetwork, joinery, boat building, musical instruments, lead pencils, cigar boxes, plywood and decorative veneers.
Workability: Generally good; difficult to bore and veneers may tend to be woolly in cutting; good bending properties.
Finishing: Fair; wood contains oils and gum which may be troublesome, but if filled, it can be brought to a smooth finish.
Weight : 30 lb./cu. ft.
Price: Moderate.

SPRUCE, SITKA
(S)

Botanical Name: *Picea sitchensis*

Sitka spruce, the largest species of spruce, can grow more than 200 feet high with diameters exceeding six feet. Although it is probably most valued for newspaper production because of its whiteness, its strength and workability make it a favorite in woodworking and construction. It is also a very resonant wood and is widely used in all types of string and keyboard instruments. Sitka spruce is often quartersawn.

Other Names: Silver spruce, sequoia silver spruce, tideland spruce, Menzies spruce, coast spruce, western spruce and west coast spruce.

Sources: Canada, U.K. and U.S.A.

Characteristics: Straight grain; medium, even texture; white to yellowish-brown with a slight pinkish tinge. Very high strength-to-weight ratio.

Uses: Interior joinery, musical instruments, boat building, oars, rowing sculls, gliders, plywood, construction and veneers.

Workability: Good; very good bending properties.

Finishing: Accepts finishes well.

Weight: 28 lb./cu. ft.

Price: Moderate.

SYCAMORE, AMERICAN
(H)

Botanical Name: *Platanus occidentalis*

Growing to heights that top 200 feet, this species and tulip poplar are the largest hardwoods in eastern North America. With its light greenish-gray bark, American sycamore is a prominent presence in any forest, and is sometimes called the ghost tree. When quartersawn, this timber possesses a distinctive fleck figure. Used to a great extent in furniture, American sycamore occasionally is rotary cut for veneers.

Other Names: American planetree, buttonwood, plane tree, water beech.

Sources: Eastern and central U.S.A.

Characteristics: Usually straight grain; fine, even texture; pale reddish-brown.

Uses: Furniture, joinery, butcher's blocks, and veneers.

Workability: Generally good; may bind on saws; maintain very sharp cutting edges; high shrinkage with a tendency to warp.

Finishing: Accepts finishes well.

Weight: 35 lb./cu. ft.

Price: Inexpensive.

TEAK
(H)

Botanical name: *Tectona grandis*

Teak is one of the most valuable woods in the world, possessing high strength and durability, along with exceptional beauty. Harvesting this precious timber presents an interesting dilemma. Freshly cut teak is so heavy that it will not float, so trees must be girdled and left to die and dry for up to three years before loggers can float them down river to the mill. The teak's leaves, the largest of any tree, possess a natural abrasiveness and are used locally as sandpaper.

Other Names: Eyun, sagwan, teku, teka.

Sources: Burma, Southeast Asia. Also grown as plantation trees in the Caribbean, East and West Africa.

Characteristics: Straight to wavy grain; coarse texture; oily surface; uniform golden brown to rich brown with deep brown markings.

Uses: Shipbuilding, interior and exterior furniture and joinery, cabinetmaking, flooring, plywood and veneers.

Workability: Satisfactory; extreme blunting of cutters due to high silica content; pre-bore for nailing; difficult to glue; sawdust is skin irritant.

Finishing: Accepts oil finishes especially well.

Weight: 40 lb./cu. ft.

Price: Expensive.

TORNILLO
(H)

Botanical Name: *Cedrelinga catenaeformis*

Tornillo is a large, relatively common tree found mainly in Peru and Brazil. Locally, this timber is used as a substitute for the over-harvested mahogany, and today it is the number one sawn lumber in Peru, where there is one well-managed source. The wood is stable, decay resistant and very attractive, and is slowly making its way into the North American market.

Other Names: Cedrorana (Brazil); Achapo (Colombia).

Sources: South America, primarily Peru and Brazil.

Characteristics: Straight to irregular grain, occasionally wavy; medium to coarse texture; heartwood pink to golden brown; sapwood off-white.

Uses: Furniture, turning, carving, and general construction and carpentry.

Workability: Generally good; blunts cutters moderately; maintain very sharp cutters for planing irregular grain.

Finishing: Accepts most finishes well.

Weight: 30-40 lb./cu. ft.

Price: Moderate.

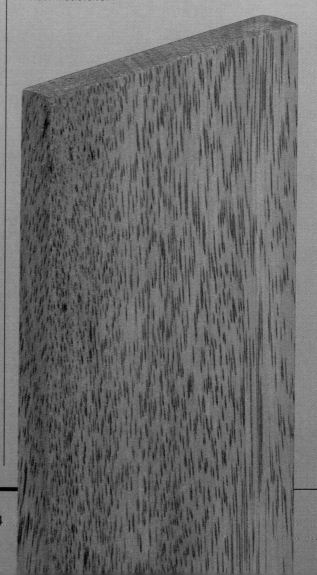

TULIPWOOD
(H)

Botanical Name: *Dalbergia frutescens*
This is an extremely valuable timber, lighter in color than any other rosewood, normally available in small cuttings only. Like all rosewoods, it grows very slowly and needs centuries for the heartwood to develop top-quality color. Because of its poor availability, tulipwood is not usually used in solid form, but as veneer for inlay on fine pieces. When it is worked, this wood tends to splinter and, like many of the rosewoods, gives off a fragrant aroma.
Other Names: Brazilian pinkwood, pinkwood (U.S.A.); pau de fuso, jacaranda rosa (Brazil).
Source: South America.
Characteristics: Irregular grain; medium-fine texture; rich golden-pinkish hue with salmon to red stripes.
Uses: Turning, brush backs, woodware, jewelry boxes, cabinetwork, inlay work, inlaid bandings, marimba keys, decorative veneers for inlay work and marquetry and antique repairs.
Workability: Difficult; extreme dulling of cutters; pre-bore for nailing.
Finishing: Accepts finishes very well; can be brought to a high natural polish.
Weight: 65 lb./cu. ft.
Price: Very expensive.

WALNUT, BLACK
(H)

Botanical name: *Juglans nigra*
Owing to its great beauty and good working characteristics, black walnut is one of the most valuable native woods in North America. Since colonial times, its wide range of figures has graced the finest American cabinetwork. Although known for its workability, walnut does contain juglone, a chemical believed to cause dermatitis in some woodworkers.
Other Names: American black walnut, American walnut, Virginia walnut (U.K.); walnut, Canadian walnut.
Sources: Eastern U.S.A. and Ontario, Canada.
Characteristics: Tough wood of medium density; generally straight grain; medium coarse texture; dark brown to purplish black.
Uses: Fine furniture, gunstocks, interior joinery, cabinetmaking, turning, boat building, musical instruments, clock cases, carving, plywood, paneling and veneers.
Workability: Good; blunts cutters moderately; good bending properties.
Finishing: Accepts natural wood finishes especially well.
Weight: 40 lb./cu. ft.
Price: Moderate.

WENGE
(H)

Botanical Name: *Millettia spp.*

A strong, heavy, hard wood, wenge offers a familiar combination to the woodworker. It is difficult to work, but delightful to look at. Originating from a tree of moderate size, this deep brown and black wood can offer distinctive veneers with characteristic light streaks of parenchyma, a tree tissue involved in food storage and consumption. For best results, wenge should be worked with very sharp cutters.

Other Names: Dikela, mibotu, African palisander.

Sources: Equatorial Africa (Cameroon, Gabon, Zaire).

Characteristics: Heavy, dense wood; straight grain; coarse texture; dark brown with blackish veins and sometimes streaked with fine, light brown lines.

Uses: Turning, interior and exterior joinery, cabinetmaking, paneling and decorative veneers.

Workability: Generally good; blunts cutting edges rapidly; pre-bore for nailing; poor bending properties.

Finishing: Satisfactory; must be filled for good results.

Weight: 55 lb./cu. ft.

Price: Moderate.

WILLOW
(H)

Botanical Name: *Salix nigra*

While its European cousin is used most notably in cricket bats, black willow is most frequently used in North America by school woodworking shops; it is the most commercially valuable of the more than 100 types of native North American willows. Willow's strength and relative lightness make it the clear choice for artificial limbs.

Other Name: Black Willow.

Sources: Canada, Eastern U.S.A. and Mexico.

Characteristics: Light, tough wood; straight grain; fine texture; grayish-brown with reddish-brown streaks.

Uses: Artificial limbs, toys, wickerwork, baskets, boxes, crates, decorative veneers.

Workability: Satisfactory; maintain sharp cutters to prevent fraying; poor bending properties; often contains reaction wood.

Finishing: Accepts finishes well.

Weight: 26 lb./cu. ft.

Price: Inexpensive.

ZEBRAWOOD
(H)

Botanical Name: *Microberlinia brazzavillensis*
Distinctive in appearance, zebrawood comes from two species of large trees found mainly in Cameroon and Gabon, West Africa. While it is usually seen as a veneer in North America, when quartersawn this timber can give beautiful results in solid form. Zebrawood is difficult to work, however, and veneers tend to be fragile.
Other Names: Zingana (France, Gabon); Allen ele, amouk (Cameroon); zebrano.
Source: West Africa.
Characteristics: Wavy to interlocked grain; medium to coarse texture; heartwood pale yellow brown with thin darker streaks; sapwood white.
Uses: Turning, tool handles, skis, inlay, furniture, cabinetwork and decorative veneers.
Workability: Fair; dulls cutting edges moderately; interlocked grain will tend to tear; suffers from high shrinkage and may be unstable in use. Flat-cut boards hard to dry.
Finishing: Fair; may be difficult to finish because of interlocked grain.
Weight: 45-50 lb./cu. ft.
Price: Expensive.

ZIRICOTE
(H)

Botanical Name: *Cordia dodecandra*
A stunning, dark wood, ziricote is easy to work and can be brought to a very smooth finish. Though difficult to dry, once this is achieved it is relatively stable and highly durable. Like bocote, ziricote is a Central American member of the cordias. The two woods are, in fact, quite similar, differing mainly in color.
Other Name: Cordia.
Sources: Belize, Mexico.
Characteristics: Straight grain, medium to moderately fine texture; black, gray or dark brown with black streaks.
Uses: Furniture, cabinetwork, interior joinery and veneers.
Workability: Very good; little blunting of cutters.
Finishing: Accepts finish well.
Weight: 45-50 lb./cu. ft.
Price: Expensive.

GLOSSARY

A-B

Absolute humidity: A measure of the weight of water vapor per unit volume of air, usually expressed as grains per cubic foot; see *relative humidity*.

Air-dried lumber: Dried lumber that has reached its equilibrium moisture content by exposure to the air.

Angiosperm: Belonging to the botanical sub-phylum or group of woody plants that have encapsulated seeds such as a walnut or acorn; includes all hardwood tree species.

Annual growth ring: The visible layer of growth that a tree puts on in a single year, including the earlywood and the latewood; seen in the end grain of wood.

Bark: The outermost layer of a tree's trunk that protects the inner wood and cambium from the elements; composed of the outer, dead cork and the inner, living phloem.

Bird's-eye figure: Figure on plainsawn and rotary-cut surfaces of a few species of wood—most commonly maple—exhibiting numerous small, rounded areas resembling birds' eyes; caused by local fiber distortions.

Blister figure: Figure on plainsawn or rotary-cut surfaces that looks like various-sized elevated and depressed areas of rounded contour.

Board foot: A unit of wood volume measurement equivalent to a piece of wood 1 inch thick, 12 inches wide and 12 inches long.

Bookmatch: In veneering, a decorative pattern in which successive veneers in a flitch are arranged side-by-side in a mirror formation, like pages of an opened book.

Bound water: Moisture present in wood found within the cell walls; see *free water*.

Bow: A lumber defect in which a board is not flat along its length.

Bucking: Crosscutting a tree into logs of a desired length.

Burl veneer: Highly decorative veneer taken from bulges or irregular growths that form on the trunks of some species and on the roots of others.

Butt veneer: Veneer cut from the area in a tree's trunk just above the roots; also known as *stump veneer*.

C

Cambium: A layer of actively growing tissue, one cell thick, between the phloem and the sapwood, which repeatedly divides itself to form new cells of both.

Cant: A log that has been debarked and sawn square in preparation for further cutting.

Case hardening: A lumber defect resulting from drying a board too rapidly; the outer layers of a board are in compression while the inner layers are in tension.

Cell: The smallest unit of wood structure, each with its own specialized function; cells include vessels, fibers, rays, and tracheids.

Check: A lumber defect in which splits develop lengthwise across the growth rings during seasoning because of uneven shrinkage of wood.

Clear: Describes a board face that is free of defects.

Common grade lumber: In softwood, lumber with conspicuous defects such as red or black knots and pith.

Compression wood: Reaction wood formed on the undersides of branches and leaning or crooked stems of softwood trees.

Conifer: Any of several families of softwood trees that bear cones; see *softwood*.

Crook: A lumber defect where there is an edgewise deviation from end-to-end straightness in a board.

Crossband: In plywood with more than three plies, the veneers immediately beneath the surface plies are oriented with a grain direction perpendicular to that of the surface plies.

Cross grain: Generally, lumber in which the wood fibers deviate from the longitudinal axis of the board; see *spiral grain*.

Cross section: A viewing plane in wood identification seen in the end grain of lumber, cut perpendicular to the axis of the tree trunk; also known as a *transverse* section.

Crotch veneer: Veneer cut from the fork of a tree trunk.

Crown-cut veneer: Decorative veneer that is cut from flitches using the flat-slicing method.

Cup: A lumber defect in which the face of a board warps and assumes a cup-like shape.

Curly grain: See *wavy grain*.

Cutting list: A list of the sizes of lumber needed for a specific project.

D-E

Deciduous: Any of several families of trees that shed their foliage annually; see *hardwood*.

Defect: Any abnormality or irregularity that lowers the commercial value of wood by decreasing its strength or affecting its appearance; see *warp*.

Dendrochronology: The science of dating past events and changes in environmental conditions by comparative study of annual growth rings.

Diamond match: In veneering, a decorative pattern formed when successive veneers from the same flitch, usually with a diagonal stripe figure, are arranged in a diamond shape.

Diffuse-porous wood: Hardwoods in which the pores tend to be uniform in size and distribution throughout each annual growth ring.

Earlywood: The portion of the annual growth ring formed in the early part of the growing season; see *latewood*.

Equilibrium moisture content: The moisture content that wood eventually reaches when it is exposed to a given level of relative humidity and temperature.

Extractive: Resins and other substances deposited in the heartwood during a tree's growth that impart both color and resistance to decay.

F-G
Face veneer: Veneer used for the exposed surfaces in hardwood and softwood plywood.

Fiber: A specific hardwood cell type, elongated with narrow ends and thick walls; contributes to the strength of the wood.

Fiber saturation point (FSP): A condition in which wood cell cavities are free of all water, yet the cell walls remain fully saturated.

Fiddleback: An attractive figure resulting when wood with curly or wavy grain is quartersawn; commonly used in the manufacture of stringed instruments.

Figure: In the broadest sense, the distinctive pattern produced in a wood surface by the combination of annual growth rings, deviations from regular grain, rays, knots, and coloration.

Finish grade lumber: Softwood lumber graded for appearance, not strength, seasoned to a moisture content of 15 percent or less; includes superior and prime categories.

Firsts and seconds: The top or premium grade of hardwood.

Flat-sliced veneer: Veneer that is sliced off a log or a flitch with a veneer slicer.

Flitch: A section of a log cut to extract the best figure and yield of veneers from a log; also known as a cant.

Free water: Moisture present in wood found inside the cell cavities; see *bound water*.

Grade stamp: A stamp applied to most softwood and some hardwood lumber indicating the grade, strength properties, species of wood and the mill that manufactured it.

Grain: Generally, the direction, size, arrangement, appearance, or quality of the elements in wood or lumber; specifically, the alignment of wood fibers with respect to the axis of the tree trunk.

Green lumber: Freshly sawn, unseasoned lumber having a moisture content above the fiber saturation point.

Gymnosperm: A botanical sub-phylum or group of woody plants that have exposed seeds like a pine seed; includes all softwood tree species.

H-I-J-K-L
Hardboard: A type of manufactured board with smoother surfaces than particleboard, made by breaking waste wood down into its individual fibers, mixing them with adhesives, and mat-forming them into a strong, homogenous panel.

Hardwood: Generally, wood from angiosperm tree species.

Headsaw: The large bandsaw or circular saw at a mill that cuts logs into large slabs of timber for resawing; also known as headrig.

Heartwood: The dead, inner core of a tree extending from the pith to the sapwood, usually distinguishable from sapwood by its darker color.

Herringbone match: In veneers, a decorative match created when successive veneers from one flitch, usually with a diagonal stripe, are arranged to form a herringbone pattern.

Humbolt undercut: A method of felling trees where a wedge is cut in the stump of a tree rather than in the upper log before it is felled.

Hygroscopicity: The ability of a substance to readily absorb, retain, and desorb moisture.

Interlocked grain: Wood that features repeated alternation of left- and right-hand deviations of fibers from the axis of the tree trunk, usually over several growth rings; results in ribbon figure on quarter-sawn surfaces.

Key: A master list of wood species used in identification, ordered by criteria such as gross anatomical features, macroscopic features, or microscopic features.

Kiln: A heated chamber used in drying lumber, veneer, or wood products where temperature, humidity, and air circulation are controlled.

Kiln-dried lumber: Lumber that has been dried to a specific moisture content.

Knot: The base of a branch or limb that has been overgrown by the expanding girth of the trunk or other portion of the tree.

Latewood: The portion of the annual growth ring formed in the latter part of the growing season; see *earlywood*.

Lesser-known species (LKS): Woods recently introduced to the market, such as chactacote, tornillo and chontaquiro amarillo, many of which come from sources that practice sustainable forest management.

Linear foot: A measurement referring only to the length of a piece of wood; see *board foot*.

Lumber: Logs that have been roughly sawn into timbers, resawn, planed and sawn to length.

Lumber-core plywood: Plywood in which softwood and hardwood veneers are glued to a core of narrow, sawed lumber.

Lumber ruler: A tool used to measure the board-foot volume of a piece of lumber, with a flexible wooden shaft and a hook for turning boards.

Luthier: A builder of stringed musical instruments such as violins and guitars.

M-N-O

Macroscopic features: Referring to anatomical features of wood identification visible with low-power magnification, typically a 10x hand lens.

Marquetry: Decorative inlay work done with veneers, metals or other materials.

Medium density fiberboard (MDF): A type of tempered hardboard with a fine texture used in cabinetmaking.

Moisture content: The amount of water contained in wood, expressed as a percentage of the weight of the oven-dried wood.

Mottled figure: A type of broken stripe figure with occasional interruptions of curly figure.

Nominal size: The rough-sawn commercial size by which lumber is known and sold.

Non-porous wood: Wood devoid of vessels, or pores; softwood.

Oven-dried weight: The constant weight of wood that has been dried in an oven at temperatures between 214° and 221° F. to a point where it no longer contains moisture.

P-Q

Parenchyma: Thin-walled cells in wood; responsible for the storage of carbohydrates. *See ray.*

Particleboard: A type of manufactured board made by breaking waste wood down into small particles, mixing them with adhesives, and extruding or mat-forming them into panels of varying thickness.

Particleboard-core plywood: Plywood in which hardwood and softwood veneers are glued to a particleboard core for added strength.

Phloem: The inner bark, which distributes nutrients derived from photosynthesis in the leaves.

Photosynthesis: A process by which plants synthesize carbohydrates and other nutrients from water and minerals in the presence of cholorphyll and sunlight.

Phylum: A botanical group or class of plants.

Pitch pocket: A pocket found within the grain of some conifers, containing an accumulation of liquid or solid resin.

Pith: The small, soft core occurring in the structural center of a tree trunk.

Plain-sawn lumber: Lumber that has been sawn so that the wide surfaces are tangential to the growth rings; also known as *flat-sawn* lumber when referring to softwood; see *quartersawn lumber.*

Plywood: A manufactured board consisting of an odd number of layers or plies of softwood or hardwood veneer; may also be made with a solid core, see *lumber-core plywood.*

Pore: A cross-section of a vessel as it appears on a transverse section of wood; see *vessel.*

Porous wood: Wood that has vessels, or pores, large enough to be seen with a hand lens; hardwood.

Quarter-cut veneer: A veneer created by slicing a flitch to expose the quartersawn surface of the wood.

Quarter match: A decorative veneer pattern created by arranging successive veneers from the same flitch, usually with a burl or crotch figure in a circular or oval formation; also known as four-way center and butt.

Quartersawn lumber: Lumber that has been sawn so that the wide surfaces intersect the growth rings, at angles between 45° and 90°; also known as vertical-grained lumber when referring to softwood; see also *plain-sawn lumber.*

Quilted figure: A distinctive, blister-like figure found in bigleaf maple.

R

Radial section: A viewing plane in wood identification cut across the grain perpendicular to the growth rings and parallel to the wood rays; the plane that extends along the axis of the tree trunk from pith to bark.

Radial shrinkage: Shrinkage that occurs across the growth rings as wood dries.

Ray: A ribbon-shaped strand of cells extending across the grain from pith to bark that appear as streaks on quartersawn surfaces; sometimes referred to as medullary ray.

Reaction wood: A lumber defect caused by stresses in leaning tree trunks and limbs; known as compression wood in softwood, and tension wood in hardwood; characterized by compressed growth rings and silvery, lifeless color.

Relative humidity: The ratio of the water vapor present in the air to the amount that the air would hold at its saturation point, usually expressed as a percentage figure; see *absolute humidity.*

Resin canal: Vertical passages between wood cells in conifers that conduct natural resins and pitch.

Ribbon figure: Distinctive vertical bands of varying luster found on quartersawn boards of wood with interlocked grain.

Riftsawn lumber: Lumber whose growth rings are at angles between 30° and 60° to the board face; also known as bastard-sawn lumber.

Ring-porous wood: Hardwoods in which the pores are comparatively large at the beginning of each annual growth ring, and decrease in size toward the outer section of the ring, forming distinct zones of earlywood and latewood.

Roe figure: Figure formed by short stripes less than 1 foot in length, found on quartersawn surfaces of woods with interlocked grain.

Rotary-cut veneer: A continuous sheet peeled from a log or flitch by rotating it on a lathe against a stationary knife.

S-T-U
Sap: The water in a tree, including any dissolved nutrients and extractives.

Sapwood: The outer portion of a tree's trunk extending from the heartwood to the cambium; distinguishable from the heartwood by its lighter color.

Sawyer: The person at a sawmill whose job it is to "read" a log before it is cut and select the appropriate cutting patterns.

Seasoning: The process or technique of removing moisture from green wood to improve its workability.

Selects: In softwood, defect-free lumber graded for clear appearance rather than strength, separated into firsts and second, C select and D select grades. In hardwood, selects is one grade below firsts and seconds.

Semi-diffuse porous wood: Wood with pores exhibiting the clear distinction between earlywood and latewood that is lacking in diffuse-porous wood, yet not so pronounced a difference as that shown by ring-porous wood; also known as semi-ring porous wood.

Slipmatch: In veneering, a repeated decorative pattern created by laying successive sheets of veneer from a flitch side-by-side.

Softwood: Generally, species from the families of trees that have a primitive cell structure, bear cones and for the most part have needle-like leaves; wood produced by softwood trees.

Solar kiln: A kiln that dries lumber with solar energy.

Sound: Describes a board face free of defects that would weaken the wood.

Specific gravity: The ratio of the weight of a wood sample to that of an equal volume of water.

Spermatophyte: Any of a phylum or group of higher plants that reproduce by seed; includes almost all tree species.

Spiral grain: A form of cross grain caused by the spiral alignment of wood fibers in a standing tree.

Stain: A discoloration in wood caused by fungi, metals, or chemicals.

Sticker: A piece of wood, usually ¾- to 1-inch thick, used to separate boards of lumber in a drying stack to permit air circulation.

Substrate: A piece of plywood, softwood or hardwood used in veneering as a core.

Surfacing: The way lumber has been prepared at a mill before it goes to a lumberyard. Also known as dressing.

Sustainable forest management: The process of managing forest land to ensure future productivity and maximize the flow of forest products without placing undue strain on the physical and social environment.

Tangential section: A viewing plane in wood identification cut along the grain tangential to the growth rings; plain-sawn lumber is sawn tangentially.

Tangential shrinkage: Wood shrinkage that occurs tangentially to the growth rings.

Tension wood: Reaction wood formed occasionaly on the upper side of branches and leaning or crooked stems of hardwood trees.

Texture: Refers to the size of the cells in wood, indicated by adjectives from fine to coarse; often confused with *grain*.

Tracheid: Long, fibrous cells that conduct sap and help support the tree.

Twist: A defect caused by the turning or winding of the edges of the board, so that one corner twists out of plane.

V-W-X-Y-Z
Veneer: A thin layer or sheet of wood sawn, sliced or rotary cut from a log or flitch.

Veneer-core plywood: Plywood that consists of three or more plies of veneers, each laid at right angles to each other with respect to grain direction.

Veneer press: A commercial or shop-built press used to apply veneers to substrates.

Vessel: Wood cells of comparatively large diameter found in hardwoods, set one atop the other to form a continuous tube for conducting water and sap up the trunk; when viewed in cross-section, vessels appear as pores.

Warp: A lumber defect or distortion of a piece of wood; see *bow, crook, cup,* and *twist.*

Wavy grain: Grain resulting from repeated, undulating right and left deviations in the alignment of wood fibers from the axis of a tree's trunk; also known as *curly grain.*

INDEX

ACKNOWLEDGMENTS

The editors wish to thank the following:

UNDERSTANDING WOOD
Delta International Machinery, Guelph, Ont.; Sheila Foley, Council of Forest Industries of B.C., Vancouver, B.C.; Jim Gundy, Appalachian Hardwood Manufacturers Assn., High Point, NC; Haddon Tool, Chicago, IL; Richard Jagels, Dept. of Forest Biology, University of Maine, Orono, ME; Lee Valley Tools Ltd., Ottawa, Ont.; Doug MacCleery, Forest Inventory and Planning, U.S. Dept. of Agriculture, Washington, DC; Duncan McTaggert, MacMillan Bloedel, Vancouver, BC; David Mitchell, Centennial Academy, Montreal, Que.; Jack Pitcher, National Hardwood Lumber Assn., Memphis, TN; Woodcraft Supply, Parkersburg, WV

SELECTING LUMBER
Les Bois M & M ltée., St-Mathieu, Que.; Jim Carse, A & M Wood Specialty Inc., Cambridge, Ont.; Communication Masters, Norcross, GA; Delta International Machinery, Guelph, Ont.; Dave Doucette, Highland Hardwoods, Brentwood, NH; Hitachi Power Tools U.S.A. Ltd., Norcross, GA; Roger Landreville, Montreal, Que.; Jack Pitcher, National Hardwood Lumber Assn., Memphis, TN; Bob Sabastina, National Hardwood Lumber Assn., Memphis, TN; Tom Searles, American Lumber Standards Committee, Germantown, MD.; Shopsmith, Inc., Montreal, Que.

VENEERS AND MANUFACTURED BOARDS
Adjustable Clamp Co., Chicago, IL; Delta International Machinery/Porter Cable, Guelph, Ont.; Lee Valley Tools Ltd., Ottawa, Ont.

DRYING AND STORING WOOD
Lee Valley Tools, Ottawa, Ont.; Bill Simpson, U.S. Forest Products Lab, Madison, WI;

WOOD DIRECTORY
A & M Wood Specialty Inc., Cambridge, Ont.; Pete Atkinson, World Conservation Monitoring Centre, Cambridge, England; R.S. Bacon Veneer Co., Hillside, IL; Tom Barrett, General Woods and Veneers, Montreal, Que.; Jim Carse, A & M Wood Specialty Inc., Cambridge, Ont.; John Curtis, The Luthier's Mercantile, Healdsburg, CA; Michael Fortune, Toronto, Ont.; Réjean Garand enr., St-Rémi, Que.; Debbie Hammel, Scientific Certification Systems, Inc., Oakland, CA; Bruce MacBryde, U.S. Fish and Wildlife Service, U.S. Dept. of the Interior, Washington, DC; Gary Meixner, Pittsford Lumber, Pittsford, N.Y; Mark Platin, Wildwoods Co., Arcata, CA; John Shipstad, Woodworkers Alliance for Rainforest Protection, Coos Bay, OR

The following persons also assisted in the preparation of this book:

Adrienne Bertrand, Elizabeth Cameron, Donna Curtis, Lorraine Doré, Graphor Consultation, Marie-Josée Harcc, Carolyn Jackson, Leonard Lee, Edna and William Mills, Brian Parsons, Maryo Proulx

PICTURE CREDITS

Cover Robert Chartier
6, 7 Mark Tucker
8, 9 Bob Anderson
10, 11 Bob Anderson
12 Courtesy Western Wood Products Association
13 Gloria H. Chomica/Masterfile
17 Bob Anderson/Masterfile
18 Ed Gifford/Masterfile
19 Erik Borg
20 Al Harvey/Masterfile
21 Courtesy Western Wood Products Association
22 Erik Borg
23 Erik Borg (2)
33 Courtesy U.S. Forest Products Laboratory (2)
36 Courtesy Better Built Corporation
40 Philip C. Jackson
60 Courtesy David R. Webb Co., Inc.
78 Erik Borg